D0897987

COMPARATIVE MYTHOLOGY

COMPARATIVE MYTHOLOGY

[Friedrich] Max Müller

ARNO PRESS

A New York Times Company

New York / 1977

Editorial Supervision: LUCILLE MAIORCA

———◆———

Reprint Edition 1977 by Arno Press Inc.

Reprinted from a copy in the John G. White
  Department, Cleveland Public Library

INTERNATIONAL FOLKLORE
ISBN for complete set: 0-405-10077-9
See last pages of this volume for titles.

Manufactured in the United States of America

———◆———

Library of Congress Cataloging in Publication Data

Miller, Friedrich Max, 1823-1900.
   Comparative mythology.

   (International folklore)
   Reprint of the 1909 ed. published by G. Routledge,
London.
   Includes index.
   1. Mythology.   I. Title.   II. Series.
BL311.M8 1977   291.1'3   77-70612
ISBN 0-405-10111-2

COMPARATIVE MYTHOLOGY

AN ESSAY

BY

PROFESSOR MAX MÜLLER

EDITED, WITH ADDITIONAL NOTES AND AN
INTRODUCTORY PREFACE ON SOLAR
MYTHOLOGY, BY

A. SMYTHE PALMER, D.D.

LONDON
GEORGE ROUTLEDGE AND SONS, LIMITED
NEW YORK: E. P. DUTTON AND CO.

Printed by BALLANTYNE, HANSON & Co.
At the Ballantyne Press, Edinburgh

CONTENTS

INTRODUCTION

₊ Notes by the Editor are enclosed within square brackets, thus [ ].

THE essay of the accomplished philologist here reprinted aroused a large amount of interest when it first appeared, and certainly deserves the appellation of 'epoch-making' with more justice than in most cases, where that much-abused word is employed. It was the pioneer essay which opened out paths of research hitherto untrodden ; the seed-corn from which has sprung a rich growth of works dealing with mythology and the history of religions. It was, above all things, stimulating. When Max Müller came as a stranger to England, in the middle of the nineteenth century, and adopted it as the home of his choice, he brought with him a singularly cultured mind, steeped in the lore of ancient India, Greece, and Rome. He had proposed the study of the Vedâs to himself as his life's work, but he could not resist the temptation of diverging into the paths of folk-lore, philology, and allied subjects into which his main theme incidentally led him. These *parerga* or side-issues he pursued with rare genius and originality, and set off with the graces of a beautifully picturesque and lucid style of which he was master. His English for a foreigner is quite marvellous.

The comparative method had been already applied with signal effect to the study of philology. It remained for Max Müller to bring it to bear on the kindred subjects of mythology, folk-lore, and religion. The papers which he threw off from time to time in reviews and literary journals, and were afterwards gathered up in the four volumes of his *Chips from a German Work-shop*, were a revelation to many readers of a new and fascinating branch of inquiry. These papers, charming in their presentment, imparted often recondite information which few scholars of that time possessed.

The present Essay on Comparative Mythology appeared in the *Oxford Essays* of 1856, a repertory of university lucubrations which in that and the following years afforded a domicile to the views and researches of writers who had yet to make their mark. Most of these were naturally of fugitive interest, and certainly none of equal importance to that here presented.

Max Müller, as is well known, was the redoubtable champion and exponent of the solar theory of mythology, which of recent years has suffered eclipse. It has been thought that in the enthusiasm of a discoverer he made exaggerated claims on its behalf, as if it were the master-key which would open every door. As a French critic sarcastically put it, ' Tous les dieux, nous savons, sont le soleil.' The extravagant lengths to which the master's ideas were pushed by an injudicious disciple, Sir George W. Cox, unhappily afforded too much ground for the ridicule which came to be heaped upon them. The solar theory has certainly been brought into disrepute by the rashness of its supporters, and from this shade it has hardly yet emerged. A contemporary skit, provoked by the wild suggestions of Sir George W. Cox, shows with what scepticism, not unwarranted, it was received. It appeared in *Kottabos*, the terminal magazine of Trinity College, Dublin, No. 5, 1870, and is attributed to the lively pen of the late Dr. R. F. Littledale. I have thought it worth reprinting as an appendage to this introduction. I believe, however, that there is now a reaction taking place in favour of the views advanced by Max Müller. Later investigations into the origins of primitive religious belief in Babylonia, Egypt, Western Asia, and America go far to justify the solar theory, and prove that the sun was verily and, indeed, the central object of early religious thought as he is of our physical system. It may not be out of place briefly to review here some of the evidence which tends to establish this conclusion.

Beyond question the noblest and most perfect symbol of power and beneficence known to man in the physical world is that marvellous creation of the Almighty ' His Sun,' the source of light, which imparts life and health and warmth and comfort to all the children of earth, the lord and ruler of the natural universe. He is 'the ultimate and single source of power,' says Tyndall, ' from which all energy is derived.' He controls all the watery vapours of the atmosphere, drawing them up on high and precipitating them in rain and snow. The mechanical power of every river that runs into the sea, the reciprocation of the tides, the force of the winds, the growth of trees and vegetables, the support of animal life are all from him. The cause of all fertility, as his name implies—Sun, ' the generator '— he ripens the corn-fields and orchards, clothes the plains with verdure, invests the sky and earth with manifold tints of beauty, ministers food and sustenance to the countless tribes of animated nature, and maintains the circularity of the seasons and of all that elaborate machinery of ebb and flow which renders this earth a fit home for its inhabitants. It cleanses and purifies as it shines, and, by the kindly cheering influences which it exercises on the feelings of the heart and powers of the intellect, possesses a stimulus which is not less moral than physical. Lapped in the warm sunshine, calm and sweet, one closes his eyes and feels himself enfolded all round by the sensible love of the great All-Father, with a comfortable assurance that no other phenomena can afford.

' Most glorious orb ! that wert a worship, ere
The mystery of thy making was reveal'd !
Thou earliest minister of the Almighty !
Which gladden'd, on their mountain tops, the
    hearts
Of the Chaldean shepherds, till they pour'd
Themselves in orisons ! Thou material God !
And representative of the Unknown—
Who chose thee for his shadow ! Thou chief
    star !
Centre of many stars ! which mak'st our earth
Endurable, and temperest the hues
And hearts of all who walk within thy rays !
Sire of the seasons ! Monarch of the climes,
And those who dwell in them ! '
        —Byron, *Manfred*, Act. iii. sc. 2.

The more one learns of this heavenly luminary from the revelations of science, the more awe-struck is he by its amazing potency and magnificence. There is nothing else in the universe of created things which so intensely arouses our wonder and admiration. The scientist who knows most of its enormous significance will be the first to bow his head before this dazzling symbol of the Infinite,

' Bowing lowly down before thee,
Thee the god-like, thee the changeless, in thine
    ever-changing skies.' [1]

[1] Tennyson's *Akbar's Dream*, Hymn I.

Men are bound to venerate with divine honours the best and highest that they know, and inasmuch as the

> ' Divinest object which th' uplifted eye
> Of mortal man is suffered to behold '

is the bountiful ' heart-cheering Sun,' it is *a priori* to be expected that pious men of old, feeling after God and striving after some worthy conception of Him, should have discarded idols and hailed His most adequate manifestation in this glorious agent, which everything proclaimed to be his vicegerent. It is always the most elevated races among the heathens that were devoted to the worship of the sun, and it would be strange indeed if it were otherwise. We may say, as Sir Arthur Helps did in case of the Incas of Peru, ' it was inevitable.' When the Creator, in the words of the Hebrew Psalmist, ' set His glory in the skies ' (Ps. viii. 1), men must have been blind indeed if they did not recognise the revelation. It carried its own evidence.

' Believe we ought this sun to be the very life and (to speak more plainly) the soule of the whole world, yea, and the principal governance of nature: and no less than a god or divine power, considering his works and operations. . . . Most excellent, right singular he is, as seeing all and hearing all. For this, I see, is the opinion of Homer (the prince of learning) as touching him alone.'

—Pliny, *Nat. Histoire*, 1634, i. 3 (trans. P. Holland).

' Was not the sunrise to man the first wonder, the first beginning of all reflection, all thought, all philosophy ? Was it not to him the first revelation, the first beginning of all thought, of all religion ? To us that wonder of wonders has ceased to exist, and few men now would even venture to speak of the sun, as Sir John Herschel has spoken, calling him " the Almoner of the Almighty, the delegated dispenser to us of light and warmth, as well as centre of attraction, and as such the immediate source of all our comforts, and, indeed, of the very possibility of our existence on earth " ' (*Chips*, iv. 178).

' No sensible object in the world,' says Dante, ' is more worthy to be made an example of the Deity than the sun, which with sensible light enlightens first itself and then all celestial and elementary bodies.'— *Convito*, p. 115.

The mystical theosophist Jacob Böhme, commenting on ' the Sun as the Centre of Natural Life,' says :—

' God effects this beneficent ministry especially through the sun, which, as a true image of the divine heart of love, governs the whole visible world and restrains the fury of the dark world.'

' The godhead, the divine light, is the centre of all life, and thus in the revelation

of God the sun is the centre of all life'
(*Signat*, 4, 17).

'God the Father creates love from his
heart; and thus the sun also indicates his
heart. It is the outer world, the figure of
the eternal heart of God, which gives
strength to all existence and life' (*Signat*,
4, 39).

'This world has a special god of nature,
namely, the sun. But he takes his existence
from the fire of God, and this again from the
light of God. Thus the sun gives the power
to the elements, and these to the creatures
and productions of the earth' (*Sechs Theos,
Punkte*, 4, 13).

As we might anticipate, the poets, who
are the seers that give expression to the
finer thoughts which all men think, have
understood sympathetically the attitude of
mind which led to religious veneration of
the day-god. Southey, for example, when
he says :—

'I marvel not, O Sun, that unto thee
In adoration man should bow the knee,
And pour his prayers of mingled awe and love ;
For like a god thou art, and on thy way
Of glory sheddest, with benignant ray,
Beauty and life and joyance from above.'

Similarly the poet of the *Seasons :*—

'Thou, O Sun !
Soul of surrounding worlds ! in whom best seen
Shines out thy Maker ! may I sing of thee ?
—Thomson, *Summer, sub. init.*

And so the mystic seer :—

' Look on the rising Sun : there God does live,
  And gives His light, and gives His heat away,
And flowers and trees and beasts and men
    receive
Comfort in morning, joy in the noonday.'
          —W. Blake, *The Sixth Black Day.*

And Milton :—

' O thou that, with surpassing glory crown'd,
Look'st from thy sole dominion, like the god
Of this new world.'
          —*Paradise Lost*, iv. 32–35.

The sun holds a prominent position in the pantheon of the aboriginal tribes of America. ' The mysterious one of day,' as this orb was called by the Dakotas, frequently appears in the myths as the father of the race of men, as the divinity which watches their progress, lends them aid, and listens to their prayers. The Algonquin word, *kesuk*, sun, is derived from a verb which means ' to give life '; expressed in the Zuñian myths by the figure that ' the sun formed the seed-stuff of the world.' It was a symbol of the divinity, the ' wigwam of the Great Spirit,' and when questioned as to whether they prayed to it they answered, ' Not to the sun, but to the Old Man who lives there.' [1]

In a precisely similar manner the Old

[1] D. G. Brinton, *Myths of the New World*, 3rd ed., pp. 163–64. But see his qualifying remarks, pp. 165–67.

Welsh bards proclaimed the sun to be ' the abode of God,' or ' heaven.' [1]

Mr. William Watson, with the divining instinct of the poet, probably gives a true expression of the primeval point of view when he sings :—

' O bright irresistible lord,
We are fruit of Earth's womb, each one,
And fruit of thy loins, O Sun,
Whence first was the seed outpoured.
To thee as our Father we bow,
Forbidden thy Father to see,
Who is older and greater than those, as thou
Art greater and older than we.'
 —*Hope of the World, and other Poems,* 1898.

Indeed, the poets are often aroused to enthusiasm when they sing the praises of this prototype of Apollo, the god of song.

In the joyous prologue which Bishop Gawin Douglas prefixed to the twelfth book of Virgil's *Æneid* (1553), he thus greets the sun as lord of May :—

' Welcum the lord of licht and lampe of day,
Welcum fosterare of tendir herbis grene,
Welcum quhikkynnar of flurist [blooming]
    flouris schene,
Welcum support of every rute and vane [vein],
Welcum confort of al kind frute and grane,
Welcum the birdis beild [shelter] apoun the
    brere,
Welcum maister and reulare of the yere,
Welcum welefare of husbandis at the plewis,

[1] Jeuan Tir Jarll, *Barddas,* i. 262.

Welcum reparare of woddis, treis, and bewis [boughs],
Welcum depaynter of the blomyt medis,
Welcum the lyffe of euery thing that spredis,
Welcum storare [steward] of al kynd bestial,
Welcum be thy bricht bemes gladand al,
Welcum celestiall myrrour and espye,
Atteiching [reproving] all that hantis sluggardy.'
            —P. 403, ll. 37–51 (ed. 1710).

There is good reason to believe that those nations of antiquity who gave worship to the heavenly bodies regarded them as only symbols of certain divine and spiritual beings who actuated and illumined them. For instance, in the Babylonian Creation Epic, *Enuma Elish*, it is said of Marduk the Creator—

' He made the stations (*matztzaruti*) for the great gods,
The stars, their likenesses (*mashalu*), in constellations (or signs) he placed.'
            —*Tab.* v., ll. 1, 2,

that is to say, the stars are the ' halves,' counterparts or representatives of the gods, not the gods themselves.

In a similar way the sun, in that most ancient of languages the Akkadian, is called *Kassêba* (in Semitic Babylonian, *tsalam*), the symbol, image, or likeness [1]—we may, no doubt, add ' of the Deity,' to complete the sense. And it was in this sense most probably that the most thoughtful of the heathen

[1] R. Brown, *Primitive Constellations*, i. 345 (*cf.* 351).

offered their devotions to the sun, and that even the Hebrew Psalmist, when he sought for an exalted image of the Most High as the source of light and life to His people, was content to say, ' The Lord God is a Sun ' (Ps. lxxxiv. 11).

When St. Callistratus, who lived 300–350, inquired of certain heathens with wonder how they came to worship the works of God's hands, they answered him that ' the sun is the god of gods, because he gives light,' and that ' the stars are images of the gods.' [1]

For the invisible things of Him—even His eternal power and Godhead—may be understood by the things that He made (Rom. ii. 20), and He has made nothing in His Creation so great and glorious as this minister of His, which does His will as His vicegerent, the lord and giver of life in the material world. In Assyrian Shamash is the name of the sun as ' one who serves,' or ' ministers,' to the God of heaven.

It was probably from some such considerations that the Greek Fathers regarded heliolatry as an excusable form of worship, provisionally and temporarily permitted to the heathen by God in the time of ignorance which He winked at, intending it to be a part of their upward education and a stepping-stone to higher things. Thus we

[1] F. Conybeare, *Monuments of Early Christianity*, p. 328.

find Justin Martyr saying, ' God formerly gave the sun as an object of worship, as it is written [Deut. iv. 19].'—*Dialogue with Trypho*, ch. cxxi. And similarly Clement of Alexandria : ' He gave the sun and the moon and the stars to be worshipped, which God (the Law says) made for the nations that they might not become altogether atheistical, and so utterly perish.'—*Stromateis*, bk. vi. ch. 14. ' Some of them, however, did not turn away from the worship of the heavenly bodies to the Maker of them, for this was the way given to the nations to rise up to God by means of the worship of the heavenly bodies. But those who would not abide by these objects assigned to them fell away to stocks and stones ' (*Ibid.*). The Israelites were warned not to degenerate to the level of the heathen who worshipped the sun and the moon and stars, and the whole host of heaven ' which Jehovah thy God has assigned (or allotted) unto all the peoples under the whole heaven.'[1]

Even in the days of Tertullian some Christians, as he tells us, were noticed to move their lips in adoration towards the rising of the sun (*Apologia adversus Gentes*, xvi.), and still later, in the fifth century, Leo the Great had occasion to complain that certain Christians before entering the Basilica of St. Peter's were accustomed to turn and

[1] See Fried. Delitzsch, *Babel and Bible*, ed. Johns, p. 270.

b

bow to the rising sun (*Sermo viii., in Natal. Dom.*), a custom condoned which still survives in the ritual of most churches.[1] M. Elisée Reclus says that many a time a French peasant, uncovering his head and pointing with his finger to the sun, has said to him in solemn tones, ' There is our God ! ' [2] Such ' sancta simplicitas ' reminds us of the *Cantico del sole* of St. Francis, in which he sang : ' Praised be my Lord God with all His creatures, and specially our brother the Sun, who brings us the day, and brings us the light ; fair is he and shining with a very great splendour ; to us, O Lord, he signifies Thee.' Philo, who regarded the heavenly bodies as ' visible and sensible deities,' recognised a type of God in the sun as the centre of all light (*De Somn.* i. 13) ; and Ammonius speaks of ' some who revere the type of the true God in the sun, and worship the life-giving principle in that type, which, so far as can be done by a perceptible object representing an invisible essence, scatters through the universe with mysterious splendour some radiance of the grace and glory that abide in His presence.' [3]

If the story be true that Voltaire, beholding the rising of the sun from a mountain top, was so overpowered by the magnificence of the spectacle that he fell on his knees and

[1] See E. B. Tylor, *Primitive Culture*, ii. 294–96, 3rd ed.
[2] *Histoire d'une Montagne*, p. 247.
[3] See J. Oakesmith, *Religion of Plutarch*, p. 73.

cried, ' O Dieu, je crois en Toi; je crois en
Toi ! '—if Turner, that ' sun-worshipper of
the old breed ' (as Ruskin termed him), a
few days before he died, exclaimed as the
setting rays fell upon his face, ' The Sun is
God ! '—if Mirabeau in his last hours, gazing
on the rising sun of spring, gave utterance
to the words, ' Si ce n'est pas là Dieu, c'est
du moins son cousin-germain ! ' it is hardly
a thing to be surprised at that men in a
state of nature have felt the potent attraction of that glorious orb and have hailed it
as the fount and source of divine life and
illumination. Job had felt the fascination
of it when he repudiated the idea for himself,
' If I beheld the sun when it shined . . .
and my heart hath been secretly enticed, or
my mouth hath kissed my hand ' (in adoration, xxxi., 26, 27). Indeed, almost in every
land where the sun has shined he has found
his votaries. The Akkadians, the Babylonians, the Arabs, the Syrians, the Canaanites, the Ancient Indians, the Egyptians, the
Persians, the Tartars, Mongols, Lapps, and
Finns, the Samoyeds, the Scandinavians, the
Aztecs, the Mexicans, the Hindus, the North
American Indians, in fact, mankind in general
from China to Peru, all have paid the homage
of their devotion to the grandest object in
creation as the worthiest surrogate of the
great Unseen Spirit. And so we find that
the Pharaohs, the Emperors of China, the
Rajahs of India, the Incas of Peru, and

other mighty kings have been content to hold their suzerain power as delegated to them by the sovereign sun whom they represented upon earth. The crowns which monarchs are proud to place upon their heads as the symbols of their power are only survivals of the radiate coronet which originally represented the shining splendour of the sun ; the *varenô*, or light of sovereignty, which rested upon the Persian kings, came from the same source. As samples of the feelings with which he inspired his worshippers, the following may be quoted. An Akkadian hymn to Shamash thus addresses him :—

' Lord, illuminator of the darkness,
    Cheerer of the sickly face ;
Merciful God, who setteth up the fallen,
    Who helpeth the meek. . . .
They make obeisance of the head, as they gaze,
    O Light of the midday sun.'
        —See Sayce, *Hibbert Lectures*, 171.

In five Chaldean Hymns to the sun as a god, translated by François Lenormant, occur the words :—

' He who establishes truth in the thoughts of the nations is thyself.
Thou knowest truth ; thou knowest what is false.'   —*Records of the Past*, xi. 124.

' Thou who annihilatest falsehood, who dissipatest evil influences.'   —*Ibid.*, 127.

The Ancient Egyptians gave the sun as a title *neb maat*, the lord of fixed law and of the unerring order of the cosmos. The following Hymn to the Aten or Sun-disk has been translated by Mr. F. Ll. Griffiths :—

' How many are the things which thou hast made :
Thou createst the land by thy will ; thou alone,
With peoples, herds, and flocks,
Everything on the face of the earth that walketh
    on its feet,
Everything in the air that flieth with its wings,
In the hills from Syria to Kush, and the plain
    of Egypt,
Thou givest to every one his place, thou framest
    their lives,
To every one his belonging, reckoning his length
    of days.'
      —[Petrie, *History of Egypt*, ii. 215 *seq.*]

Among the Ancient Persians, *Mihr*, the friendly sun, was called the loving and merciful, because he cherishes and refreshes the whole world and embraces it, as it were, in his love. The widespread development of this conception in the Mithraism of later times need only be referred to. Hyde, *Historia Religionis Veterum Persarum*, whom I am here quoting (p. 105), adds that the Gavri (Giaours), though they prostrate themselves before the rising sun, are not idolaters. ' They offer homage to it as the most perfect creature which God has made. They say that God has placed His throne in it, and therefore its glorious majesty deserves the lowliest veneration. Accordingly they offer their salutation to the rising sun, and even the Armenian Christians crossing themselves do the same ' (p. 106). The modern Parsis entertain ideas very similar, holding that God is most conspicuous in flame, and speaks to them still in fire as He did to Moses in time of old.[1]

Mr. C. L. Brace, in his beautiful book *The Unknown God*, quotes a Yasht of the Zend Avesta, which says, ' He who offereth up a sacrifice unto the undying, shining, swift-horsed Sun to withstand darkness . . . offereth it to the Lord Omniscient ' (p. 195).

This hidden meaning of sun-worship is thus unfolded by Browning :—

' The sun rode high. " During our ignorance "—
Began Ferishtah—" folk esteemed as God
Yon orb : for argument, suppose him so—
Be it the symbol, not the symbolised,
I and thou safelier take upon our lips.
Accordingly, yon orb that we adore
—What is he ? Author of all light and life :
Such one must needs be somewhere : this is he.
Like what ? If I may trust my human eyes,
A ball composed of spirit-fire, whence springs
—What, from this ball, my arms could circle round?
All I enjoy on earth. By consequence
Inspiring me with—what ? Why, love and
      praise." '
      —Browning, ' Ferishtah's Fancies,' *Works*,
            1900, vol. ii. p. 663.

---

[1] See Draper, *Intellectual Development of Europe*, i. 97.

When a Jesuit priest preached to the Moluches, they replied : ' Till this hour we never knew nor acknowledged anything greater than the sun.' The Shawnees in North America used the same argument, namely, that the sun animates everything, and therefore must be the master of life, or the Great Spirit. There was a considerable amount of truth in Scheffer's dictum, ' Every god of the heathen is only the sun regarded according to his different mode of working ' (*Cœlum Poeticum*, 1646, p. 33). See M. Müller's chapter on ' Solar Myths ' (*Chips*, iv. 287–327), in which he demonstrates that ' as certainly as the sun, with all that is dependent on it, forms the most prominent, half-natural, half-supernatural object in the thoughts of the ancient and even of the modern world, are solar myths a most important ingredient in the language, the tradition, and the religion of the whole human race.' Mr. Tylor, he says, has shown that ' there are solar myths wherever the sun shines (*Ibid.*, p. 198). See his work on *Primitive Culture*, i. 290 *seq.* ; ii. 285–96. The many gods of the Egyptian religion seem to be only varying phases of the Sun-god Ra, and many savages who have adored the sun have confessed that they pierced beyond to a higher divinity, who gave him light.

When the Emperor Akbar, one of the earliest students of comparative religion, questioned the Brahmins as to their tenets, they told him that the sun being the greatest of lights, the primary origin of everything, even of the royal power, it was only proper that they should worship and reverence him. The very lives of men depended upon him.[1] In the Western world we find the sun proclaimed to be the Lord and Master of the Roman Empire—'Sol Dominus Imperii Romani,'[2]—and its coins and banners testified its devotion to the all-conquering luminary, 'Soli Invicto.'

It is well known with what enthusiasm the Emperor Julian, in his effort to resuscitate paganism, paid homage to 'King Sun' as 'the first of the gods' and 'King of the Universe.'[3]

It is noticeable that most of his worshippers personalised the sun as a righteous Judge who witnessed the actions of men and read the thoughts of their hearts. As the source of law and order (*rita*), he imparted to the Babylonian King Hammurabi (about 2000 B.C.) the earliest code for governing men's conduct.

'Nor did the ancient Bard
Amiss believe, that Sol with seeing eye
Surveyed the world, but also with an ear

---

[1] See M. Müller, *Science of Religion*, pp. 95, 96.
[2] See Hochart, *La Religion Solaire dans l'Empire Romain*; Saintyves, *Les Saints Successeurs des Dieux*, p. 356.
[3] H. Rendall, *The Emperor Julian*, pp. 78, 79.

This orb endued, as if therein he saw
A type of Him who heareth e'en our thoughts.'
    —J. B. Morris, *Nature : A Parable,*
        bk. ii. ll. 429–33.

The Apache Indian points to the sun and says to the white man, ' Do you not believe that this deity sees our actions and chastises us if they are wicked ' (Froebel). A Huron woman hearing the perfections of God extolled by a Christian priest exclaimed, ' I had always pictured to myself our Areskui (the sun and the great spirit) as of the nature which you ascribe to your God ' [Lafitau, *Mœurs des Sauvages Ameriquains,* i. 127].— O. Peschel, *The Races of Man,* p. 254.[1]

The Dakota Indian prays to the sun, in which a Manitou or Great Spirit lives, and says, ' Wahkan Ate ! onshemada ! '—' Sacred Spirit, Father ! have mercy on me.'—M. C. Judd, *Wigwam Stories of North American Indians,* p. 94.

' When the Indians saw the power of the sun in bringing life out of the earth in the shape of growing plants from hidden seeds, the sun seemed to them like a living spirit.' —*Ibid.,* p. 219.

To these savages the sun was as real and living a person as Helios was to the Homeric Greeks, and we know that the later Hellenes repudiated the blasphemous materialism of those philosophers who denied the divinity and personality of what they regarded to be

[1] See E. B. Tylor, *Primitive Culture,* i. 290, 3rd ed.

only a red-hot ball of metal. Both Greek and Roman agreed in calling the sun to witness when any flagrant breach of divine law was toward. The last act of the dying was to turn in trust and hope to the rays of the sun as a religious duty ; [1] even as the evening hymn of the Christian poet, 'Sun of my soul' (=Assyrian *Shamash-napishtim*), was inspired by the sight of the setting orb of day.

M. Müller, in his *Origin and Growth of Religion*, writing of the sun as a supernatural power, notes that the Vedic poets looked upon Sûrya, the sun, as the divine leader of all the gods, as the ruler, establisher, and creator of the world ; as the defender and kind protector of all things living ; as one who knows all things, even the thoughts of men—in fact, as a divine or supreme being. He is even implored to deliver man from sin. The prayer which goes up from the many millions of the Hindu race every day —the Gâyatrî—is this : ' Let us meditate on the adorable splendour of Savitri (" the life-giving " sun) ; may he arouse our minds ' (pp. 264–70).

In the case of the ancient Egyptians a parallelism between Ra and his worshipper was traced which naturally resulted in the personification of the sun as a being like to himself.[2] The experiences of the two in

[1] Euripides, *Alcestis*, ll. 207–8 ; *Hecuba*, l. 435.
[2] See further Budge, *Egyptian Religion*, p. 121 *seq ;* M. Müller, *Contributions to Mythology*, p. 172 *seq ;* Ragozin, *Chaldæa*, p. 338 *seq.*

life, death, and resurrection, were believed
to be identically the same.

' As soon as the Egyptian began to think,
he perceived the most obvious of the simi-
larities between the sun's career and that of
man.   Man has his dawn and setting.   Man
grows from the early glimmerings of infancy
to the apogee of his wisdom and strength ;
he then begins to decline, and, like the
magnified evening sun, ends by disappearing
after his. death into the depths of the soil.
In Egypt the sun sets every evening behind
the Libyan chain :   thence he penetrates
into those subterranean regions of Ament,
across which he has to make his way before
the dawn of the next day.   The Egyptiàn
tombs were therefore placed on the left
bank of the Nile—that is, in the west of the
country.   All the known pyramids were
built in the west, and there we find all the
more important " cities of the dead," the
necropolis of Memphis, and those of Aby-
dos and Thebes.   " To the west ! to the
west ! " was the cry of the mourners in the
funeral procession.   Each morning sees the
sun arise as youthful and ardent as the
morning before.   Why, then, should not man,
after completing his subterranean journey
and triumphing over the terrors of Ament,
cast off the darkness of the tomb and again
see the light of day.   This undying hope was
revived at each dawn as by a new promise,
and the Egyptians followed out the analogy

by the way in which they disposed their sepulchres. They were placed in the west of their country, towards the setting sun, but their doors, the openings through which their inmates would one day regain the light, were turned towards the *East*. In the necropolis of Memphis the door of nearly every tomb is turned toward the East, and there is not a single stele which does not face in that direction. . . . Thus from the shadowy depths where they dwell, the dead have their eyes turned to that quarter of the heavens where the life-giving flame is each day re-kindled, and seem to be waiting for the ray which is to destroy their night and to rouse them from their long repose.' [1]

There is every reason to believe that the earliest hopes of humanity as to resurrection, a future life, and immortality were suggested by the teachings of the solar drama, and it might be shown that there is a fundamental no less than a superficial connection between the words ' East ' and ' Easter ' as well as the conceptions which they embody.

From the considerations above mentioned it appears that

' the golden sun in splendour likest heaven '

of all natural objects drew to itself a predominant share of men's worship and

[1] Perrot-Chipiez, *Art in Ancient Egypt*, i. 156–57.

religious reverence, in all times and in every nation under heaven. Seeing that there is no other created thing which can at all compare with its resplendent orb as an adequate symbol of the Divine, in its beauty and beneficence and marvellous power, it is only what we might *a priori* expect as extremely probable that the sun should play a prominent part, in one form or another, in the myths of all peoples who had eyes to see, minds to comprehend, and hearts to feel his influence. The preponderance of probable truth lies on the side of those who maintain—the onus of disproof on those who minimise or deny—the prevalence of the solar element in mythology.

A. SMYTHE PALMER.

THE OXFORD SOLAR MYTH

A CONTRIBUTION TO COMPARATIVE MYTHOLOGY

(Dedicated, without permission, to the Rev. G. W. Cox, M.A.)

A VERY singular tradition, possibly due to the influence of classical Paganism in the course of study, still preserves, in the Oxford of the nineteenth century, the evident traces of that primeval Nature-worship whereby the earliest parents of the Aryan race marked their observance of the phenomena of the heavens. As so often occurs, the myth has assumed a highly anthropomorphic and concrete form, has gradually been incrusted with the deposits of later ages, and has been given a historical or rather a biographical dress, which thereby veils, under modern names and ideas of the West, the legends current four thousand years ago on the table-lands of Trans-oxiana.

The legend takes its not infrequent shape of celebrating a great teacher, passing from his Eastern birthplace on to the West, making his home therein, achieving great triumphs, and yet succumbing, in his chiefest struggle, to a power mysteriously identical with that which gave him being. The symbolical name by which the hero was deified, even in our own days, is Max Müller. The purely imaginative and typical character of this title appears at the first glance of a philologist. Max is, of course, *Maximus*, μέγιστος, identical with the Sanskrit *maha*. Müller, applied in the late High German dialects to the mere grinder of corn, denotes in its root-form a pounder or crusher. It comes from the radical *mar*, ' grinding,' or ' crushing.' At once, then, we see that the hero's name means simply ' Chief of Grinders.' There are two explanations of this given. The more popular, but less correct, one, identifies *grinder* and *teacher* [1]—a metaphor borrowed from the monotonous routine whereby an instructor of the young has to pulverise, as it were, the solid grains of knowledge, that they may be able to assimilate it. The more scientific aspect of the question recognises here the Sun-God, armed with his hammer or battle-axe of light, pounding and crushing frost and clouds alike into impalpability. We are not left to conjecture in such a matter, for the weapon of Thor or Donar, wherewith he crushes the Frost-giants, in Norse myth-

[1] At Trinity College, Dublin, *grinder* is the usual word for a ' coach.' So in Genesis iv. 22, ' instructor ' is in the Hebrew ' whetter ' (*lôtesh*, from *lêtash*, to whet or sharpen), also in Deut. vi. 7.]

ology is named *Mjölnir*, from *at mala*, ' to crush or mill.'

Thus far, however, there might be a merely accidental coincidence of name, or the title might be a hereditary one in a priestly family devoted to the Sun-god's service. We require more exact data before we can with authority allege that Max Müller is indeed the Sun, or rather the Dawn, himself. But these data are accessible and abundant. In the first place, the legends are unanimous in representing him as a foreigner, travelling from the East, but making his home in the West, and received there by all as though native to the soil. This is very important. If he were depicted as indigenous, or as coming from North, South, or West, the difficulty to be overcome, though by no means insurmountable, would be considerable. The Eastern origin, however, obviates any doubt of this nature. Next, fable has not been slow to localise his birthplace. He is invariably called a German. This looks, at first, as though merely denoting the rough way in which an untutored people is content to transfer the origin of any strange thing to the nation nearest to itself in the direction of transit, just as, even still, the inhabitants of Norway suppose storms to be sent them by the wizards of Lapland and Finland. Germany, being the nearest country to the east of England, may thus have naturally been selected as the Sun-God's birthplace; but a deeper idea seems to underlie the title. The duality of the Sun and Moon is too remarkable a phenomenon ever to have escaped popular attention; and we find them represented in almost every known mythology as brother and sister, Helios and Selene, Apollo and Artemis, Janus and Diana, and the like. Here, then, is a clue. It is not nationality, but brotherhood to the Moon which is denoted, and Müller the German is neither more nor less than the *Germanus Apollo* of Latin poets.

Again, having invented his birthplace, it was necessary, as the myth became more concrete, to provide him with a father also. The legend relates that his father was one Wilhelm Müller, a poet. Herein a very singular aspect of the solar myth, common to all its purest forms, appears. Darkness is the parent out of which the Dawn comes, a parent dethroned by its offspring, as typified in the story of Kronos and Zeus. Wilhelm is simply Will-hjælm, the 'helmet of force,' or of strength. What is this helmet? We have it over and over again in our nursery legends; as the 'cap of darkness' (*tarnkappe*) worn by Hasan of El-Basra in the 'Arabian Nights,' by Jack the Giant-killer, and by Dwarf Trolls in Norse and Teuton stories, and, above all, by Sigfrit in the Niebelungen Lied. It is thus simply the covering of clouds and obscurity

which overspreads the heavens when the
Sun has disappeared ; and William Müller
is only the Night, hidden but powerful,
the νεφεληγέρετα Ζεύς, who is father of
Apollo Helios. Night is typified as a poet,
because all sounds are heard so clearly and
distinctly during its course, just as the song
of the primeval bard was the only voice
loud enough to make itself audible in the
stillness of pre-historic ages.

The Sun-God appears next, but still in
the same relation, in his other character of
teacher and enlightener, an idea symbolised
by Max Müller editing the Vedas at the
instigation of Bunsen = *Bundes-sohn* (*vinculi
filius*), another Teutonic hero, who typifies
the offspring of that darkness which chains
the world in the prison of night. Max is
not called—and this is noteworthy—the
author of the Vedas, or books of knowledge,
but only their editor or translator. The
meaning of this is plain. Sunrise does not
create the sensible world for us at each
recurrence, but it makes it visible and
knowable by us. Bunsen sending Müller to
achieve the task is only another form of the
myth which makes Wilhelm the father of
Max.[1]

---

[1] That Max Müller is not called the *author*, but only
the *translator* or *editor* of the Vedas, has puzzled many
who have read his great work. This curious inversion
of language, so inexplicable, except to the comparative
mythologist, obtains a significance only on the principle
suggested in the text.

The next point of interest in the fable is the place where the Sun-God fixes his sacred abode. It is noteworthy that in no case do we find the special shrine of Apollo in the chief city of any land. Athens was the beloved home of Pallas Athene ; Sparta, of the Dioscuri ; Ephesus, of Artemis ; Rome, of Jupiter Optimus Maximus and Mavors Gradivus : but Apollo always chooses a smaller and more sacerdotal city as his dwelling—Delphi, Delos, Patara. So the priestly city of Oxford is, in the English legend, assigned to Max Müller. Let us see why. Ox-ford, as all philologists know, is not Βόσπορος. *Ox* is *Usk*, *uisge* = water ; and the compound word means no more than the ' ford of the river.' We shall best see its relation to the Sun-God by turning to the Edda. We find there that all the Aesir ride over the rainbow-bridge Bifröst to Valhalla, except Thor, who has to wade on foot through four rivers—Körmt, Ormt, and the two Kerlaug streams. This denotes, of course, the Sun making his way by slow degrees through the watery clouds, and at length attaining the mid-heaven.

The task of the Sun, when he has fairly begun to climb the sky, is to spread the great blue mantle over it. This mantle is woven or *stitched*, if we take the Sanskrit myth, by the Harits or Hours, the Χάριτες of the Greeks. We find it styled in poetical language the ' cope of heaven.' And by a

quaint grotesqueness of metaphor, we discover this function of the Dawn symbolised
under the formula of Max Müller being at
first Professor in the Taylorian Institution.
Taylorian here, of course, is not a patro-
nymic or eponymous adjective, but a tro-
pological epithet. In Greek mythology,
Artemis, as well as Athene, is mistress of
the loom ; but in this curious myth her
brother appears as superintending the tasks
of the divine maidens who ply their shuttle
and shape the garment of the heavens at
his command. Here, too, we find cropping
up the struggle with the powers of darkness,
Max Müller is *Taylorian ;* he cuts away
with his glittering shears the ragged edges of
cloud ; he allows the ' chips,' or cuttings
from his ' workshop,' to descend in fertilising
showers upon the earth.

But he has a foe striving to cast a black
mantle over the sky which he would fain
clothe in blue. This foe does not merely
trim or patch together the work of others,
as a *tailor*, but is the original maker of his
own product ; and thus he is symbolically
called Weber, or *weaver*. And while Max is
of more account in the West, Weber reigns
securely over the East, which the other has
quitted.

But even the Western sky is no secure
dominion. All through the earliest poetry
and the remotest legends of ancient races,
we find the note of sorrow for the decline of

day following at once on the triumphal tone which marks the ascent of the Sun to the zenith. The combat with the powers of darkness, which began with victory, is resumed, and always ends in defeat. Hence the wailing for Yanbushadh, for Thammuz or Adonis, for the Dorian Apollo, and for Baldur. The solar legend shines clearly yet through the mists in which the ignorance of our uncritical age had enveloped it. The Sun-god, fresh from his Vedas, enters upon a struggle with a competitor, apparently of the feeblest, for the throne of the sky. This throne, in the Oxford myth, is called the Boden Chair. *Boden* is not an English word. We must look to the Sun-god's home for its meaning; and we find that in the Teuton language *boden* is *floor*. Only one floor can be meant, that of which the greatest of English poets speaks :—

> ' Look how the floor of heaven
> Is thick inlaid with patines of bright gold.'

There are two most remarkable circumstances in this legend of the strife for the Boden Chair, which put its mythical origin quite beyond all doubt. In the first place, the overthrow of Max in the struggle is said by all the bards to be due, not to the result of a single combat with his adversary, wherein he must needs have been victorious, but to the gathering together at the sacred city of a number of obscurantist beings, clothed in black, and assembling from all parts of the country to secure the victory of the inferior warrior. It is almost superfluous to point out that this legend denotes no more than the black clouds assembling from all quarters of the heavens, to hide the brightness of the Sun. If any doubt yet remained, it would be dispelled by the name of the feeble victor, the Paris who slays Achilles, the Aegisthus of this Agamemnon, the Höd of our Baldur. The name given to him in the myth is Monier Williams. The intelligent reader will at once see that this is only a new aspect of the earliest part of the myth. *Monier* is, plainly enough, *meûnier, molinarius, miller* =Müller. *Williams* we had before. Monier Williams then=Wilhelm Müller ; and the father, as in the story of Sohrab and Rustum, slays his beloved son. What is this but that the Darkness, out of which the Dawn sprang in its infancy, also re-absorbs it, and hides its glory at the end of its career ? This is the reason for the singular inversion of the order of the names. At first the darkness is the primary fact, and the power it exercises only the secondary one ; and thus the helmet or *tarn-kappe* is put first, and the epithet of *grinder* or *crusher* in the lower place. But in the latter part of the myth, the slaying of the Sun-god is the earlier event, and not until that is accomplished, and the Western sky is red with his blood, does the victor put on the helmet of will, and spread darkness over the heavens.

There are consolations even in defeat. A bridal, in the mysterious life which follows death, is accomplished in the Western land ; and that legend which takes so many shapes —the marriage of Uranos and Gaea, the descent of Zeus in golden shower on Danaë, and the like—is brought before us again in the wedding of Max Müller and the mortal maiden Grenfell, who denotes the *green hill* or *mountain pasture* on which the Sun delights to shine. We have this idea of the domestic joys of Helios, even after his declension and setting, preserved for us in Greek poetry :—

> Ἀέλιος δ' Ὑπεριονίδας δέπας ἐσκατέβαινε
> χρύσεον, ὄφρα δι ὠκεανōιο περάσας
> ἀφίκοιθ' ἱερᾶς ποτὶ βένθεα νυκτὸς ἐρεμνᾶς
> ποτὶ μάτερα, κουριδίαν τ' ἄλοχον,
> παῖδάς τε φίλους.—ARCHILOCHUS.

[A later scholiast has remarked that it is not without significance that the nymph Greenfell (Greenfeld and Greenfield are other variants), who became the bride of the ' Mighty-Miller,' had the pre-nomen of Georgina ascribed to her. This is well known to be a feminine form of Geôrgos, the ' earth-worker ' or Tiller of the soil, and the dependence of the agriculturist on the fostering love of the Sun deity is plainly suggested, just as the verdure of the fields and pastures

also contained in her name is due to the
same cause.   There is no fertility apart from
the sun.   An old tradition that the mother
of the sun's spouse bore the name of Elliot
points to the same conclusion, a more correct
form being Eliot, which through loss of the
aspirate stands for Heliot.   This is mani-
festly the Greek word Ἡλιωτὶς (Hêliôtis), the
female sun, by which name the Ionians denoted the moon as the wife of the sun.
Whether Charlotte the pre-nomen of this
matron 'Eliot, to be analysed as *Charl* (*Carl*)
+*ot*, a fem. termination, is to be identified
with Latin *carrulus*, a little car, with allusion
to the sun-chariot of Phaethon, is less
obvious.   But that the earth-cultured verdure, wedded inseparably to the Sun-hero,
was borne to him by the sun-chariot of
Heliot, forms a legend sufficiently transparent.]

Thus we see the great teacher passing
from the waters to the verdant slopes, from
Oxford to Grenfell—

> φοιτᾷς δ' ὑπερπόντιος ἐν τ'
> ἀγρονόμοις αὐλαῖς.—SOPH., *Antig.* 754.

He reappears, however, if not as perennial
holder of the throne on the floor of the sky,
yet as the expounder of speech, or, in the
Euhemerist phrase of sceptics, ' Professor of
Comparative Philology.'   What are we to
understand by this title ?   No more than
that sudden awakening of the sounds of

Nature which greets the sunrise as night
vanishes with its darkness and silence.
Hence the epithet πανόμφαιος, ' Source of
all speech,' given to Zeus as Dyauspati, and
to Helios also, as in Quintus Smyrnaeus—

τόν ῥά τέ φασιν
ἔμμεναι 'Ηελίοιο πανομφαίοιο θυγατρῶν
δάκρυ.—*Posthomeric*, v. 625.

There can be no question that the meaning
' inspirer of all oracles ' is a development
of a far later age, when the meteorological
idea had been lost ; and there is a com-
paratively obscure legend which seems at
first to point in the same direction. Nothing is clearer than that the sacred city of
Oxford was the chosen shrine of the hero
Max Müller. But he appears as a passing
meteor in the annals of the other holy town
of the English land. Cambridge alleges
that for a day he was Rede Lecturer in her
halls. Cambridge is the ' cam ' or *crooked*
bridge (compare ' game ' leg, *cambuca*) of
the sky, *i.e.* the Rainbow. What is *Rede* ?
Two rival theories exist. The first sees in
the word the notion of counsel or advice.
So in the ballad of King Estmere—

' Rede me, rede me, deare brother,
My rede shall ryde at thee.'

The Rede Lecturer then will be simply
Apollo Pythius, the god of counsel, applied
to in some one sudden emergency. The
other view seems more tenable. It sees in

Rede the Norse *reidh*, a *chariot*, the Latin *rheda*, and recognises in the title *Rede-Lehrer*, not a *lecturer* at all, but Ving-Thor himself, the driver of the fiery car, whence he is called *Hlorridi*, from *at hlóa*, to glow or burn, and *reidh*.[1] [See Grimm, *T. Myth*, 187.]

[1] The identification of Cambridge with the rainbow, or curving bridge of the sky, at once simple and convincing, clears up the difficulty about Max Müller's one visit there, and his immediate return to dwell at Oxford. For the legend is in minute agreement with the Eddaic myth, which tells how Thor essayed once, and once only, to drive over Bifröst in his war-chariot, but had to desist, lest he should set the bridge on fire. He returned ever after to his wading through the four rivers of which we have spoken above ; that is, to Ox-ford. And the myth of the Sun's chariot, common to Greek legend, finally settles the meaning of *Rede*, putting the interpretation ' counsel ' out of court. Another obscure legend, quite disassociated with the Müller myth, confirms remarkably the identification of Oxford with the water, and Cambridge with the sky. There is a tradition still handed down that a strife, constantly renewed, existed between these two cities, not, as one should anticipate, in the rivalry of learning, but in some way connected with ships or boats. When so engaged, the names of Oxford and Cambridge are dropped, and those of Dark Blue and Light Blue appear in their stead. The former of these titles, applied to Oxford, points at once to the οἴνοπα πόντον, the *mare purpureum* of Greek and Latin poets, and the ' dark blue sea ' of a famous English bard, while the rival epithet, describing the lighter shade of the heavens (compare Theocritus, γλαυκὰν ναίουσαν ὑπ' ἀῶ [*Idyll*, lxvi. 5], and Ennius, *caeli caerula templa*) is applied to Cambridge, and the true meaning of the myth comes out by the reference to boats, as we thus learn that it typifies the astonishment of the first Aryans who reached the Caspian and the Persian Gulf, at the elemental strife of a storm at sea, when sky and waves seem to those in a ship to be crashing together.

' The sky, it seems, would pour down stinking pitch,
   But that the sea, mounting to the welkin's cheek,
   Dashes the fire out.'—*Tempest*, Act i. sc. 2.

Another legend, belonging to Oxford, calls Max Müller for a time by the singular title of ' Fellow (or Companion) of All Souls,' and ceases to give him this appellation after he meets with the nymph Grenfell. Here is a difficulty needing solution. Hermes, not Apollo, is the ψυχοπομπός of Greek mythology, and the epithet is one applied, in the *Alcestis*, to Charon also. It is only in the Edda that we find the answer. Odin, who is a Sun-god as well as Thor, though he usually sends the Valkyrier to conduct the souls of slain heroes to Vingolf, yet sometimes, in his character of Valfödhr, is himself the guide of such chieftains as, nobly born and clad in warriors' armour, have died with more than common valour and renown. And thus the ancient statutes of the Fellowship show that *all* souls are not meant to be honoured, but only the souls of those who are *bene nati* and *bene vestiti*, the true Einherjar of the foundation. These departed heroes are no other than the sun-beams, slain by the advancing powers of darkness, but collected again by their father, the Sun, who burns them on the glowing pile of the Western evening sky, and then revives them once more to shine in Gladsheim. The loss of this office of ψυχοπομπός on wedding a mortal is a myth which has several congeners. It is akin to that of Orpheus and Eurydice, though less tragic in its termination ; and its meaning here plainly is the return of the Sun to Earth from the unseen 'combination - room' whither his rays vanished at his setting. He returns to living nature, and is, as stated above, not any more 'Fellow of All Souls,' silent and ghostly, but Professor of all Languages, vocal and embodied. This office, however, ties him to earth ; and we find the story of Apollo's servitude to Admetus repeated ; because the task imposed on the hero is to look after the training of the young Bulls. He thus appears as Phœbus Nomios ; and a confusion between the oxytone word νομή or νόμος, *pasture*, and the paroxytone word νόμος, *law*, has led to a curious error in the Cambridge form of the myth. In this imperfect record Max Müller is styled 'Doctor of Laws,' as though he were *Thesmophoros*. But that epithet belongs properly to Dionysos :—

θεσμοφόρον καλέω ναρθηκοφόρον Διόνυσον.
—*Orphica*, xlii. 1.

[The Sun, however, was the original giver of laws, as in the case of Hammurabi, referred to above, p. xx.] And the more exact Oxonian records preserve his true title as 'Master of Arts.' This is not merely the Apollo of Parnassus, leader of the Muses, inspirer of poetry, painting, and sculpture, beautiful as such a personification is. It goes far deeper ; and we see in Max Müller, M.A., the elemental Fire-god, whose chief manifestation is the Sun, but whose heat and light are essential to all life and manufacture. And thus he is described in Aeschylus :—

τὸ σὸν γὰρ ἄνθος, παντέχνου πυρὸς σέλας.
—*Prom. Vinct.*, 7.

A fragment of a solar hymn, apparently having reference to the hero or divinity Müller, is still chanted by children in the mystic rites of the gynæceum :—

> ' There was a jolly Miller
>   Lived on the river Dee,
> And thus the burden of his song
>   For ever used to be—
>   I jump mejerrime jee !
> I care for nobody, no, not I,
>   And nobody cares for me ! '

Jolly is, of course, *Jovialis*, noting that the Müller referred to is no mortal, but the son of Jovis or Dyaus ; and the *river* is, of course, the Ox-ford (*Uisge*) through which he daily wades. He is the master of song, because the birds commence their music as he rises. *Mejerrime jee* presents great difficulty. It is clearly a trace of the primeval lay, and is as hard to explain as κόγξ ὄμπαξ. The earlier word looks Oscan, and seems to be the superlative of the root *maj*, ' great,' which we have in *maj-estas*, *major* (Spanish, *mejor*), and then, probably, *majorrimus*. The second word, most likely, stands for *age ;* and the whole phrase denotes the quick leap of the levin-brand from the cloud. The interpretation Μεγαρικὴ γῆ, though ingenious, is untenable. And in the two closing lines, wherein some have thought the disposition of a human Max Müller to be exactly pourtrayed, those who, with truer science, acknowledge him to be a solar myth, will recognise that grand impassive inexorability of natural phenomena which at once strikes and awes every untutored man as well as every civilised philosopher

It is not easy to overrate the interest and value of such a legend as this to the comparative mythologist Few solar myths are so detailed and various, and, perhaps, there is none which brings together in so concentrated a focus the special characteristics of Sanskrit, Hellenic, and Norse fable.

COMPARATIVE MYTHOLOGY

Phædros. Dost thou see that very tall plane-tree ?

Sokrates. Certainly I do.

Phædros. There is shade there, and the wind is not too strong, and there is grass to sit, or, if we like, to lie down.

Sokrates. Lead on then !

Phædros. Tell me, Sokrates—is it not from some place here they say that Boreas carried away Oreithyia from the Ilissos ?

Sokrates. So they say.

Phædros. Should it not be from this spot ? for the waters seem so lovely, and pure, and transparent, and as if made for girls to play on the bank.

Sokrates. No ; it is two or three stadia further down, where you cross over to the Temple of Agra—and there you find, somewhere, an altar of Boreas.

Phædros. I was not aware of this. But tell me, by Zeus, O Sokrates—doest *thou* believe this myth to be true ?

Sokrates. Well, if I did not believe it, like the wise people, I should not be so very far wrong ; and I might set up an ingenious theory and say that a gust of Boreas, the Northwind, carried her down from the rocks in the neighbourhood, while she was playing with her friend Pharmakeia ; and that, having died in this manner, she was reported to have been carried off from thence by Boreas, or from the Ares peak

A

—for there goes also this story, that she was carried off from that, and not from this spot. As to myself, Phædros, I think these explanations, on the whole, very pleasant ; but they require a man of strong mind and hard work, and a man who, after all, is not much to be envied, if it were only for this, that when he has set right this one fable, he is bound to do the same for the form of the Hippokentaurs, and again for that of the Chimæra. And then a host of such beings rushes in—Gorgons and Pegasos, and masses of other hopeless beings, and absurdities of monstrous creatures. And if a man, not believing in the existence of these creatures, should try to represent each according to the probable explanation, dealing in a rough kind of philosophy—he would require abundance of leisure. I, at least, have no time to spare for these things, and the reason, my friend, is this—that I cannot yet, according to the Delphic line, know myself ; and it seems to me ridiculous that a man who does not yet know this, should trouble himself about what does not concern him. Therefore I leave those things alone, and, believing what other people believe about them, I meditate, as I said just now, not on them, but on myself—whether I be a monster more complicated and more savage than Typhon, or a tamer and simpler creature, enjoying by nature a blessed and modest lot. But while we are talking, my friend—was not this the tree to which thou wert to lead us ?

Phædros. This is the very tree.

THIS passage, from the Introduction of Plato's *Phædros*, has been frequently quoted in order to show what the wisest

of the Greeks thought about the rationalists
of his day. There were at Athens then, as
there have been at all times and in all
countries, men who had no sense for the
miraculous and supernatural, and who,
without having the moral courage to deny
altogether what they could not bring themselves to believe, endeavoured to find some
plausible explanation by which the sacred
legends which tradition had handed down
to them, and which had been hallowed by
religious observances, and sanctioned by the
authority of the law, might be brought into
harmony with the dictates of reason and the
laws of nature. That Sokrates, though ac-
cused himself of heresy, did not entertain
a very high opinion of these speculators
—that he thought their explanations more
incredible and absurd than even the most
incredible absurdities of Greek mythology—
nay, that at a certain period of his life he
treated such attempts as impious, is clear
from this and other passages of Plato and
Xenophon.

But if Mr. Grote, in his classical work
on the *History of Greece*, avails himself of
this and similar passages, in order to intro-
duce, as it were, Sokrates himself among
the historians and critics of our own time—
if he endeavours to make him bear witness
' to the uselessness of digging for a supposed
basis of truth' in the myths of the Greek
world, he makes the ancient philosopher

say more than he really said. Our object in considering the myths[1] of the Greeks, or any other nation of antiquity, is so different from that of Sokrates, that the objections which he urged against his rationalising contemporaries could hardly be said to apply to us. Nay, I believe it can be shown that, from our point of view, their study forms part of that very problem the solution of which Sokrates considered to be the only worthy object of philosophy. For what is it that makes us at the present day ask the question of the origin of the Greek myths ? Why do men study ancient history, acquire a knowledge of dead languages, and decipher illegible inscriptions ? What inspires them with an interest not only in the literature of Greece and Rome, but of ancient India and Persia, of Egypt and Babylonia ? Why do the puerile and often repulsive legends of savage tribes rivet their attention and engage their thoughts ? Have we not been told that there is more wisdom in the *Times* than in Thukydides ? Are not the novels of Walter Scott more amusing than Apollodorus ? or the works of Bacon more instructive than the cosmogony of the Purânas ? What, then, gives life to the study of antiquity ? What compels men,

---

[1] [This word was still imperfectly naturalised when M. Müller wrote in 1856, as here and throughout the essay he writes it " mythe." The pronunciation *meith*, rhyming with *blithe*, may still be heard occasionally.]

in the midst of these busy times, to sacrifice
their leisure to studies apparently so un-
attractive and useless, if not the conviction,
that in order to obey the Delphic command-
ment—in order to know *what Man is*, we
ought to know *what Man has been ?* This
is a view as foreign to the mind of Sokrates
as any of the principles of inductive philosophy by which men like Columbus,
Leonardo da Vinci, Copernicus, Kepler,
Bacon, and Galileo regenerated and in-
vigorated the intellectual life of modern
Europe. If we grant to Sokrates that the
chief object of philosophy is that man should
know himself, we should hardly consider
his means of arriving at this knowledge
adequate to so high an aim. To his mind
man was pre-eminently the individual, the
human soul by itself, without any reference
to its being but one manifestation of a
power, or, as he might have said, an idea,
realised in and through an endless variety
of human souls. He is ever seeking to
solve the mystery of human nature by
brooding over his own mind, by watching
the secret workings of the soul, by analysing
the organs of knowledge, and by trying to
determine their proper limits ; and thus the
last result of his philosophy was, that he
knew but one thing, and this was, that he
knew nothing. To us, man is no longer
this solitary being, complete in itself, and
self-sufficient ; man to us is a brother

among brothers, a member of a class, of a genus, or a kind, and therefore intelligible only with reference to his equals. The earth was unintelligible to the ancients, because looked upon as a solitary being, without a peer in the whole universe ; but it assumed a new and true significance as soon as it rose before the eye of man as one of many planets, all governed by the same laws, and all revolving around the same centre. It is the same with the human soul, and its nature stands before our mind in quite a different light since man has been taught to know and feel himself as a member of one great family—as one of the myriads of wandering stars, all governed by the same laws, and all revolving around the same centre, and all deriving their light from the same source. The history of the world, or, as it is called, ' Universal History,' has laid open new avenues of thought, and it has enriched our language with a word which never passed the lips of Sokrates, or Plato, or Aristotle—*man-kind*. Where the Greek saw barbarians, we see brethren ; where the Greek saw heroes and demi-gods, we see our parents and ancestors ; where the Greek saw nations (ἔθνη), we see mankind, toiling and suffering, separated by oceans, divided by language, and severed by national enmity —yet evermore tending, under a divine control, towards the fulfilment of that inscrutable purpose for which the world was

created, and man placed in it, bearing the
image of God. History, therefore, with its
dusty and mouldering pages, is to us as
sacred a volume as the book of nature. In
both we read, or we try to read, the reflex
of the laws and thoughts of a Divine
Wisdom. As we acknowledge no longer in
nature the working of demons or the manifestation of an evil principle, so we deny
in history an atomistic conglomerate of
chances, or the despotic rule of a mute fate.
We believe that there is nothing irrational
in History and Nature, and that the human
mind is called upon to read and to revere
in both the manifestations of a Divine
Power. Hence, even the most ancient
and shattered pages of traditions are dear
to us, nay dearer, perhaps, than the more
copious chapters of modern times. The
history of those distant ages and distant
men—apparently so foreign to our modern
interests—assumes a new charm as soon as
we know that it tells us the story of our own
race, of our own family—nay, of our own
selves. Sometimes, when opening a desk
which we have not opened for many years—
when looking over letters which we have not
read for many years, we read on for some
time with a cold indifference, and though we
see it is our own handwriting, and though
we meet with names once familiar to our
heart, yet we can hardly believe that *we*
wrote these letters, that *we* felt those pangs,

that *we* shared in those delights, till at last
the past draws near and we draw near to
the past, and our heart grows warm, and
we feel again as we felt of old, and we know
that these letters were *our* letters.   It is the
same in reading ancient history : at first it
seems something strange and foreign ; but
the more intensely we read, the more our
thoughts are engaged and our feelings
warmed ; and the history of those ancient
men becomes, as it were, our own history—
their sufferings *our* sufferings—their joys *our*
joys.   Without this sympathy, history is a
dead letter, and might as well be burnt and
forgotten ; while, if it is once enlivened by
this feeling, it appeals not only to the antiquarian, but to the heart of every man.
We find ourselves on a stage on which many
acts have been acted before us, and where
we are suddenly called to act our own part.
To know the part which we have to act ourselves, we ought to know the character of
those whose place we take.   We naturally
look back to the scenes on which the curtain
of the past has fallen, for we believe that
there ought to be *one* thought pervading the
whole drama of mankind.   And here history
steps in, and gives us the thread which
connects the present with the past.   Many
scenes, it is true, are lost beyond the hope
of recovery ; and the most interesting, the
opening scenes of the childhood of the
human race, are known to us by small frag-

ments only. But for this very reason the antiquarian, if he descries a relic of those early times, grasps it with the eagerness of a biographer who finds unexpectedly some scraps written by his hero when yet a child —entirely himself, and before the shadows of life had settled on his brow. In whatever language it may be written, every line, every word, is welcome, that bears the impress of the early days of mankind. In our museums we collect the rude playthings of our hero's boyhood, and we try to guess from their colossal features the thoughts of the mind which they once reflected. Many things are still unintelligible to us, and the hieroglyphic language of antiquity records but half of the mind's unconscious intentions. Yet more and more the image of man, in whatever clime we meet him, rises before us, noble and pure from the very beginning : even his errors we learn to understand—even his dreams we begin to interpret. As far as we can trace back the footsteps of man, even on the lowest strata of history, we see that the divine gift of a sound and sober intellect belonged to him from the very first ; and the idea of a humanity emerging slowly from the depths of an animal brutality can never be maintained again. The earliest work of art wrought by the human mind—more ancient than any literary document, and prior even to the first whisperings of tradition—the *human language*, forms an uninterrupted chain from the first dawn of history down to our own times. We still speak the language of the first ancestors of our race ; and this language, with its wonderful structure, bears witness against such unhallowed imputations.

The formation of language, the composition of roots, the gradual discrimination of meanings, the systematic elaboration of grammatical forms—all this working which we can still see under the surface of our own speech, attests from the very first the presence of a rational mind—of an artist as great, at least, as his work. This period, during which expressions were coined for the most necessary ideas—such as pronouns, prepositions, numerals, and the household words of the simplest life—a period to which we must assign the first beginnings of a free and simply agglutinative grammar— a grammar not impressed as yet with any individual or national peculiarities, yet containing the germs of all the Turanian,[1] as well as the Arian[2] and Semitic forms of speech—this period forms the first in the history of man—the first, at least, to which

[1] [Turanian means virtually non-Aryan, being origin ally applied to the nomad races of Asia as swift (*Tura*) horsemen. See M. Müller, *Science of Language*, 8th ed., i. 277, 334 ; H. D. Whitney, *Linguistic Studies*, 243.]

[2] [The author afterwards abandoned this spelling for the more correct " Aryan," Sansk. *Arya*, the tillers, or land-owners, which is adopted from this point.]

even the keenest eye of the antiquarian and the philosopher can reach—and we call it the *Rhematic Period.*

This is succeeded by a second period, during which we must suppose that at least two families of language left the simply agglutinative, or nomadic stage of grammar, and received, once for all, that peculiar impress of their formative system which we still find in all the dialects and national idioms comprised under the names of *Semitic* and *Aryan,* as distinguished from the *Turanian,* the latter retaining to a much later period, and in some instances to the present day, that agglutinative re-productiveness which has rendered a traditional and metamorphic system of grammar impossible, or has at least considerably limited its extent. Hence we do not find in the nomadic or Turanian languages scattered from China to the Pyrenees, from Cape Comorin, across the Caucasus, to Lapland, that traditional family likeness which enables us to treat the Teutonic, Celtic, Windic, Italic, Hellenic, Iranic, and Indic languages on one side, and the Arabian, Aramean, and Hebrew dialects on the other, as mere varieties of two specific forms of speech, in which, at a very early period, and through influences decidedly political, if not individual and personal, the floating elements of grammar have been arrested and made to assume an amalgamated, instead of a merely agglutinative character. This second is called the *Dialectical Period*.

Now, after these two periods, but before the appearance of the first traces of any national literature, there is a period, represented everywhere by the same characteristic features—a kind of Eocene period, commonly called the *Mythological* or *Mythopœic Age*. It is a period in the history of the human mind, perhaps the most difficult to understand, and the most likely to shake our faith in the regular progress of the human intellect. We can form a tolerably clear idea of the origin of language, of the gradual formation of grammar, and the unavoidable divergence of dialects and languages. We can understand, again, the earliest concentrations of political societies, the establishment of laws and customs, and the first beginnings of religion and poetry. But between the two there is a gulf which it seems impossible for any philosophy to bridge over. We call it the *Mythic Period*, and we have accustomed ourselves to believe that the Greeks, for instance, such as we find them represented to us in the Homeric poems, far advanced in the fine arts, acquainted with the refinements and comforts of life, such as we see at the palaces of Menelaos and Alkinoos, with public meetings and elaborate pleadings, with the mature wisdom of a Nestor and the cunning enterprise of an Odysseus, with the dignity of a Helena and the loveliness of a Nausikaa, could have been preceded by a race of men whose chief amusement consisted in inventing absurd tales about gods and other nondescript beings—a race of men, in fact, on whose tomb the historian could inscribe no better epigram than that on Bitto and Phainis.[1] Although later poets may have given to some of these fables a charm of beauty, and led us to accept them as imaginative compositions, it is impossible to conceal the fact that, taken by themselves, and in their literal meaning, most of these ancient myths are absurd and irrational, and frequently opposed to the principles of thought, religion, and morality which guided the Greeks as soon as they appear to us in the twilight of traditional history. By whom, then, were these stories invented ?—stories, we must say at once, identical in form and character, whether we find them on Indian, Persian, Greek, Italian, Slavonic, or Teutonic soil.

---

[1] [The epigram referred to is this :—

Βιττὼ καὶ Φαινὶς φίλη ἡμέρη, αἱ συνέριθοι,
   αἱ πενιχραὶ γραῖαι, τῇ δ' ἐκλίθημεν ὁμοῦ·
ἀμφότεραι Κῷαι, πρῶται γένος· ὦ γλυκὺς ὄρθρος,
   πρὸς λύχνον ᾧ μύθους ἥδομεν ἡμιθέων.

> *Anthologia Palatina*, cap. ii. 196 (vol. iii. p. 120, ed. Firmin Didot).

" Here poor old spinsters two, of noblest birth,
   Lie we and hail the dawn ;
We sang the stories of the demigods on earth,
   By lamplight until morn.]

Was there a period of temporary insanity, through which the human mind had to pass, and was it a madness identically the same in the south of India and in the north of Iceland ? It is impossible to believe that a people, who, in the very infancy of thought, produced men like Thales, Herakleitos, and Pythagoras, should have consisted of idle talkers but a few centuries before the time of these sages. Even if we take only that part of mythology which refers to religion, in our sense of the word, or the myths which bear on the highest problems of philosophy—such as the creation, the relation of man to God, life and death, virtue and vice—myths generally the most modern in origin, we find that even this small portion, which might be supposed to contain some sober ideas, or some pure and sublime conceptions, is unworthy of the ancestors of the Homeric poets, or the Ionic philosophers. If the swineherd Eumæos, unacquainted, perhaps, with the intricate system of the Olympian mythology, speaks of the Deity, he speaks like one of ourselves. 'Eat,' he says to Odysseus, 'and enjoy what is here, for God will grant one thing, but another he will refuse, whatever he will in his mind, for he can do all things'[1]

---

[1] *Od.* x. 443:—

Ἔσθιε, δαιμόνιε ξείνων, καὶ τέρπεο τοῖσδε
Οἷα πάρεστι· θεὸς δὲ τὸ μὲν δώσει τὸ δ' ἐάσει,
Ὅττί κεν ᾧ θυμῷ ἐθέλῃ· δύναται γὰρ ἅπαντα.

This, we may suppose, was the language of the common people at the time of Homer, and it is simple and sublime, if compared with what has been supposed one of the grandest conceptions of Greek mythology, that, namely, where Zeus, in order to assert his omnipotence, tells the gods, that if they took a rope, and all the gods and goddesses pulled on one side, they could not drag him down from the heaven to the earth; while, if he chose, he could pull them all up, and suspend the earth and the sea from the summit of Olympos. What is more ridiculous than the mythological account of the creation of the human race by Deukalion and Pyrrha throwing stones behind them (a myth which owes its origin to a mere pun on λάος and λᾶας),[1] while we can hardly expect, among pagans, a more profound conception of the relation between God and man—than the saying of Herakleitos—'Men are mortal gods, and gods are immortal men.' Let us think of the times which could bear a Lykurgos and a Solon—which could found an Areopagos and the Olympic games, and how can we imagine that, a few generations before that time, the highest notions of the Godhead among the Greeks were adequately expressed by the story of Uranos maimed by Kronos—of

[1] [It would be somewhat similar if one were to imagine a connection between Welsh *pobl*, "people," and Old English *pobble*, "pebble."]

Kronos eating his children, swallowing a stone, and vomiting out alive his whole progeny. Among the lowest tribes of Africa and America we hardly find anything more hideous and revolting. It is shutting our eyes to the difficulties which stare us in the face, if we say, like Mr. Grote, that this mythology was ' a past which was never present ; ' and it seems blasphemy to consider these fables of the heathen world as corrupted and misinterpreted fragments of a divine revelation once granted to the whole race of mankind—a view so frequently advocated by Christian divines. These myths have been made by man at a certain period of history. There *was* an age which produced these myths— an age half-way between the Dialectical Period—presenting the human race gradually diverging into different families and languages, and the National Period—exhibiting to us the earliest traces of nationalised language, and a nationalised literature in India, Persia, Greece, Italy, and Germany. The fact is there, and we must either explain it, or admit in the gradual growth of the human mind, as in the formation of the earth, some violent revolutions, which broke the regularity of the early strata of thought, and convulsed the human mind, like volcanoes and earthquakes arising from some unknown cause, below the surface of history.

Much, however, will be gained if, without

being driven to adopt so violent and re-
pugnant a theory, we are able to account
in a more intelligible manner for the creation
of myths. Their propagation and subsistence in later times, though strange in
many respects, is yet a much less intricate
problem. The human mind has an inborn
reverence for the past, and the religious
piety of the man flows from the same
natural spring as the filial piety of the
child. Even though the traditions of past
ages may appear strange, wild, and sometimes immoral, or impossible, each genera-
tion accepts them, and fashions them so
that they can be borne with again, and even
made to disclose a true and deeper meaning.
Many of the natives of India, though versed
in European science, and imbued with the
principles of a pure natural theology, yet
bow down and worship the images of
Vish*n*u and *S*iva. They know that these
images are but stone ; they confess that
their feelings revolt against the impurities
attributed to these gods by what they call
their sacred writings ; yet there are honest
Brahmans who will maintain that these
stories have a deeper meaning—that im-
morality being incompatible with a divine
being, a mystery *must* be supposed to be
concealed in these time-hallowed fables—
a mystery which an inquiring and reverent
mind may hope to fathom. Nay, even
where Christian missionaries have been suc-

B

cessful, where the purity of the Christian faith has won the heart of a native, and made the extravagant absurdities of the Purânas insupportable to him, the faith of his early childhood will still linger on and break out occasionally in unguarded expressions, as several of the myths of antiquity have crept into the legends of the Church of Rome.[1] We find frequent indications in ancient history that the Greeks themselves were shocked by the stories told of their gods ; yet as even in our own times faith with most men is not faith in God or in truth, but faith in the faith of others, we may understand why even men like Sokrates were unwilling to renounce their belief in what had been believed by their fathers. As their idea of the Godhead became purer, they also felt that the idea of perfection, involved in the idea of a divine being, excluded the possibility of immoral gods. Pindar, as pointed out by Otfried Müller,[2] changes many myths because they are not in harmony with his purer conceptions of the dignity of gods and heroes ; and because, according to his opinion, they *must*

[1] See Grimm's Introduction to his great work on *Teutonic Mythology*. Second edition, 1844, p. xxxi. [Eng. ed., vol. iii. xxxv. *seq.* Also Conyers Middleton, *Letter from Rome*, 1749 ; P. Saintyves, *Les Saints Successeurs des Dieux*, 1907 ; H. Delahaye, *The Legends of the Saints*, 1907 ; E. Lucius, *Les Origines du Culte des Saints.*]

[2] See O. Müller's excellent work, *Prolegomena zu einer wissenschaftlichen Mythologie* (1825), p. 87.

be false. Plato [1] argues in a similar spirit when he examines the different traditions about Eros, and in the *Symposium* we see how each speaker maintains that myth of Eros to be the only true one which agrees best with his own ideas of the nature of this god—Phædros [2] calling him the oldest, Agathon the youngest of the gods ; yet each appealing to the authority of an ancient myth. Thus, men who had as clear a conception of the omnipotence and omnipresence of a supreme God as natural religion can reveal, still called him Zeus, forgetting the adulterer and parricide.

' Ζεὺς ἀρχή, Ζεὺς μέσσα, Διὸς δ' ἐκ πάντα τέτυκται.'

' Zeus is the beginning, Zeus the middle ; out of Zeus all things have been made '

—an Orphic line, but an old one, if, as Mr. Grote supposes, Plato alluded to it. [3] Poets again, who felt in their hearts the true emotion of prayer, a yearning after divine help and protection, still spoke of Zeus, forgetting that at one time Zeus him-

---

[1] *Phædros*, 242, E.

[2] *Symp.* 178, C. οὕτως πολλαχόθεν ὁμολογεῖται ὁ Ἔρως ἐν τοῖς πρεσβυτάτοις εἶναι· πρεσβύτατος δὲ ὢν μεγίστων ἀγαθῶν ἡμῖν αἴτιός ἐστιν· 195, A. ἔστι δὲ κάλλιστος ὢν τοιόσδε· πρῶτον μὲν νεώτατος θεῶν, ὦ Φαῖδρε.

[3] Lobeck, *Aglaoph*, p. 523, gives

Ζεὺς κεφαλὴ Ζεὺς μέσσα Διὸς δ ἐκ πάντα τέτυκται.

See Preller's *Greek Mythology*, 1854, p. 99.

self was vanquished by Titan and delivered by Hermes.[1] Aeschylos[2] says: 'Zeus, whoever he is, if this be the name by which he loves to be called—by this name I address him. For, pondering on all things except Zeus, I cannot tell whether I may truly cast off the idle burden from my thought.'

No, the preservation of these mythic names, the long life of these fables, and their satisfying the religious, poetical, and moral wants of succeeding generations, though strange and instructive, is not the real difficulty. The past has its charms, and Tradition has a powerful friend in Language. We still speak of the sun rising and setting, of rainbows, of thunderbolts, because Language has sanctioned these expressions. We use them, though we do not believe in them. The difficulty is how at first the human mind was led to such imaginings—how the names and tales arose, and unless this question can be answered, our belief in a regular and consistent pro-

---

[1] *Apollod*, 1, 6, 3, Grote, H. G., p. 4.
[2] I give the text, because it has been translated in so many different ways :

> ' Ζεύς, ὅστις ποτ' ἐστιν, εἰ τόδ' αὐ-
> τῷ φίλον κεκλημένῳ,
> τοῦτό νιν προσεννέπω·
> οὐκ ἔχω προσεικάσαι,
> πάντ' ἐπισταθμώμενος
> πλὴν Διός, εἰ τὸ μάταν ἀπὸ φρόντιδος ἄχθος
> χρὴ βαλεῖν ἐτητύμως.'

gress of the human intellect, through all ages and in all countries, must be given up as a false theory.

Nor can it be said that we know absolutely nothing of this period during which the as yet undivided Aryan nations—for it is chiefly of them that we are now speaking —formed their myths. Even if we saw only the deep shadow which lies on the Greek mind from the very beginning of its political and literary history, we should be able to infer from it something of the real character of that age which must have preceded the earliest dawn of the national literature of Greece. Otfried Müller,[1] though he was unacquainted with the new light which comparative philology has shed on this primitive Aryan period, says, 'The mythic form of expression which changes all beings into persons, all relations into actions, is something so peculiar that we must admit for its growth *a distinct period* in the civilisation of a people.' But comparative philology has since brought this whole period within the pale of documentary history. It has placed in our hands a telescope of such power that, where formerly we could see but nebulous clouds, we now discover distinct forms and outlines ; nay, it has given us what we may call contemporary evidence, exhibiting to us the state of thought, language, religion,

[1] *Prol. Myth.*, 78.

and civilisation at a period when Sanskrit was not yet Sanskrit, Greek not yet Greek, but when both, together with Latin, German, and other Aryan dialects, existed as yet as *one* undivided language, in the same manner as French, Italian, and Spanish may be said to have at one time existed as *one* undivided language, in the form of Latin.

This will require a short explanation. If we knew nothing of the existence of Latin —if all historical documents previous to the fifteenth century had been lost—if tradition, even, was silent as to the former existence of a Roman empire, a mere comparison of the six Romance dialects would enable us to say, that at some time there must have been a language from which all these modern dialects derived their origin in common; for without this supposition it would be impossible to account for the facts exhibited by these dialects. Let us look at the auxiliary verb. We find :

	Italian.	Wallachian.	Rhætian.
I am :	sono	sum (sunt)	sunt
Thou art :	sei	es	eis
He is :	e	é (este)	ei
We are :	siamo	sŭntemu	essen
You are :	siete	sŭnteɹi	esses
They are :	sono	sŭnt	eân (sun)

	Spanish.	Portuguese.	French.
I am :	soy	sou	suis
Thou art :	eres	es	es
He is :	es	he	est
We are :	somos	somos	sommes
You are :	sois	sois	êtes (estes)
They are :	son	são	sont.

It is clear, even from a short consideration of these forms, first, that all are but varieties of one common type ; secondly, that it is impossible to consider any one of these six paradigms as the original from which the others had been borrowed. To this we may add, thirdly, that in none of the languages to which these verbal forms belong, do we find the elements of which they could have been composed. If we find such forms as *j'ai aimé,* we can explain them by a mere reference to the radical means which French has still at its command, and the same may be said even of compounds like *j'aimerai,* i.e. *je-aimer-ai,* I have to love, I shall love. But a change from *je suis* to *tu es* is inexplicable by the light of French grammar. These forms could not have grown, so to speak, on French soil, but must have been handed down as relics from a former period—must have existed in some language antecedent to any of the Romance dialects. Now, fortunately, in this case, we are not left to a mere inference, but as we possess the Latin verb, we can prove how by phonetic corruption, and by mistaken analogies, every one of the six paradigms is but a national metamorphosis of the Latin original.

Let us now look at another set of paradigms :

	Sanskrit.	Lithuanian.	Zend.	Doric.
I am :	ásmi	esmi	ahmi	ἐμμι
Thou art :	ási	essi	ahi	ἐσσὶ
He is :	ásti	esti	asti	ἐστί
We (two) are :	'svás	esva	...	...
You (two) are :	'sthás	esta	stho ?	ἐστόν
They (two) are :	'stás	(esti)	sto ?	ἐστόν
We are :	'smás	esmi	hmahi	ἐσμές
You are :	'sthá	este	sta	ἐστέ
They are :	sánti	(esti)	hĕnti	ἐντί

	Old Slavonic.	Latin.	Gothic.	Armen.
I am :	yesmĕ	sum	im	em
Thou art :	yesi	es	is	es
He is :	yestŏ	est	ist	ê
We (two) are :	yesva	...	siju	...
You (two) are :	yesta	...	sijuts	...
They (two) are :	yesta	...	...	...
We are :	yesmŏ	sumus	sijum	emq
You are :	yeste	estis	sijuth	êq
They are :	somtĕ	sunt	sind	en.

From a careful consideration of these forms, we ought to draw exactly the same conclusions ; firstly, that all are but varieties of one common type ; secondly, that it is impossible to consider any of them as the original from which the others have been borrowed ; and thirdly, that here again, none of the languages in which these verbal forms occur, possess the elements of which they were composed. That Sanskrit cannot be taken as the original from which all the rest were derived (an opinion held by many scholars) is clear, if we see that Greek has, in several instances, preserved a more primitive, or, as it is called, more organic form than Sanskrit. Εσ-μές cannot be derived from the Sanskrit *smas*, because *smas* has lost the radical *a*, which Greek has preserved, the root being *as*, to be, the termination *mas*, we. Nor can Greek be fixed upon as the more primitive language from which the others were derived, for not even Latin could be called the daughter of Greek, the language of Rome having preserved some forms more primitive than Greek ; for instance, *sunt* instead of ἐντί or ἐνσί. Here Greek has lost the radical *as* altogether, ἐντί standing instead of ἐσεντι, while Latin has at least, like Sanskrit, preserved the radical *s* in *sunt = santi*.

Hence, all these dialects point to some more ancient language which was to them what Latin was to the Romance dialects —only that at that early period there was no literature to preserve to us some remnants of that mother-tongue that died in giving birth to the modern Aryan dialects such as Sanskrit, Zend, Greek, Latin, Gothic, Windic, and Celtic. Yet, if there is any truth in inductive reasoning, that language was once a living language, spoken in Asia by a small tribe, nay, originally by a small family living under one and the same roof, as the language of Camoens, Cervantes, Voltaire, and Dante, was once spoken by a few peasants who had built their huts on the Seven Hills near the Tibris. If we compare the two tables of paradigms, the coincidences between the language of the Veda and the dialect spoken at the present day by the Lithuanian recruit at Berlin are greater by far than between French and Italian ; and, after Bopp's *Comparative Grammar* has been completed, it will be seen clearly that all the essential forms of grammar had been fully framed and established before the first separation of the Aryan family took place.

But we may learn much more of the intellectual state of the primitive and undivided family of the Aryan nations, if we use the materials which Comparative Philology has placed at our disposal ; and, here again, the Romance languages will teach us the spell by which we may hope to open the archives of the most distant antiquity of the Aryan race. If we find in all the Romance dialects a word like the French *pont*, the Italian *ponte*, the Spanish *puente*, the Wallachian *pod*, identically the same in all, after making allowance for those peculiarities which give to each its national character, we have a right to say that *pons*, the name for *bridge*, was known *before* these languages separated, and that, therefore, the art of building bridges must have been known at the same time. We could assert, even if we knew nothing of Latin and of Rome, that previous at least to the tenth century, books, bread, wine, houses, villages, towns, towers and gates, &c., were known to those people, whoever they were, from whose language the modern dialects of Southern Europe are derived. It is true, we should not be able to draw a very perfect picture of the intellectual state of the

Roman people if we were obliged to con-
struct their history from such scanty
materials ; yet, we should be able to prove
that there really was such a people, and,
in the absence of any other information,
even such casual glimpses would be welcome. But, though we might safely use
this method positively, only taking care to
avoid foreign terms, we could not convert it
or use it negatively. Because each of the
Romance dialects has a different name for
certain objects, it does not follow that the
objects themselves were unknown to the
ancestors of the Romance nations. Paper
was known at Rome, yet it is called *carta* in
Italian, *papier* in French.

Now, as we know nothing of the Aryan
race before it was broken up into different
nationalities — such as Indian, German,
Greek, Roman, Windic, Teutonic, and
Celtic—this method of making language
itself tell the history of ancient times will
become of great value, because it will give
a character of historical reality to a period
in the history of the human race, the very
existence of which had been doubted—to a
period that had been called ' a past that
was never present.' We must not expect
a complete history of civilisation, exhibiting
in full detail a picture of the times when the
language of Homer and of the Veda had not
yet been formed. But we shall feel by
some small but significant traits the real

presence of that early period in the history
of the human mind—a period which, for
reasons that will be clearer hereafter, we
identify with the *Mythopœic*.

	Sanskrit.	Zend.	Greek.	Latin.
Father :	pitár	patar	πατήρ	pater
Mother :	mâtár	mâtar	μήτηρ	mater
Brother :	bhrâtar	brâta	(φρατήρ)	frater
Sister :	svásar	khanhar	...	soror
Daughter :	duhitar	dughdhar	θυγάτηρ	...

	Gothic.	Slav.	Irish.
Father :	fadar	...	athair
Mother :	...	mati	mathair
Brother :	brôpar	brat	brathair
Sister :	svistar	svestra	siur
Daughter :	dauhtar	dukte (Lith.)	dear.[1]

[1] [The radical meaning of these family relationships
may be summed up in these doggerel rhymes :—

> '*Father* is *feeder* of the family
> As lord, or " loaf-ward," for his meinie ;
> *Mother*—called *mêtêr* anciently—
> The *meter* out of *meat* is she,
> Or " loaf-divider " now yclept ladye.
> *Sister* assister *sweet* should be,
> *Brother* the *bearer* of burdens gladly ;
> *Daughter dugs* milketh for the *dairie*.
> Their part each plays thus in the family.

Pa-ter, from *pā*, to nourish. ' We clepedh him
fader for that he *fet* (*feedeth*) alle liuende thing . . . he
fedeth and is therefore hore (their) *fader*.'—*Old English
Homilies*, 12th cent., 2nd ser., p. 25. (*Lord* for *lowerd*,
i.e. *hláf-weard*, ' loaf-keeper,' like Ger. *brot-herr*, ' bread-
master,' as *lady* for *lafdi*, i.e. *hláf-dige*, ' loaf-maker.')
Mater, *meter*, from *mā*, to measure, whence *mete* and
probably *meat*, a measured portion ; Scand. *mat-
moder*, ' food-mother ' ; *Svasar* (*swestr*) apparently
akin to *swad*, sweet, both compounded with *su*, well,
see below p. 32. *Bhrâtar* (*bhartar*) from *bhar*, to
bear. *Duhitar* from *dhugh* (*duh*) to milk (as if *ductrix*
from *duc-o*), whence also *dug* and perhaps *dairy*, i.e.
deyery, the place of the *dey* or milkmaid (cf. Ang.
Ind., *daye*, nurse ; Hind, *dāī*.]

The mere fact, that the names for *father*, *mother*, *brother*, *sister*, and *daughter* are the same in most of the Aryan languages, might at first sight seem of immaterial significance ; yet, even these words are full of import. That the name of father was coined at that early period, shows that the father acknowledged the offspring of his wife as his own, for thus only had he a right to claim the title of father. *Father* is derived from a root PA, which means, not to begét, but to protect, to support, to nourish.[1] The father as genitor, was called in Sanskrit ganitár, but as protector and supporter of his offspring he was called pitár. Hence, in the *Veda* these two names are used together, in order to express the full idea of father. Thus the poet says (1, 164, 33) :

> Dyáus me pitâ′ ganitâ′
> Jovis mei pater genitor.
> Ζεὺς ἐμοῦ πατὴρ γενετήρ.

In a similar manner mâtar, mother, is joined with ganitrî, genitrix (*Rv.* III. 48, 2), which shows that the word mâtar must soon have lost its etymological meaning, and have become an expression of respect and endearment. For among the early Aryans, mâtar had the meaning of maker, from MA, to fashion ; and, in this sense, and with the

---

[1] [So among the Semites *ab* often denoted a fosterer or protector rather than a physical begetter. See W. Robertson Smith, *Religion of the Semites*, chap. ii.]

same accent as the Greek μήτηρ, mâ'tar, not
yet determined by a feminine affix, is used
in the *Veda* as a masculine.   Thus we read,
for instance, *Rv.* VIII., 41, 4 :

' Sáh mâ'tâ pûrvyám padám.'

(He, Varu*n*a (Uranos), is the maker of the old
   place.)

Now, it should be observed, that mâtar,
as well as pitar, is but one out of many names
by which the idea of father and mother
might have been expressed.   Even if we
confined ourselves to the root PA, and took
the granting of support to his offspring as
the most characteristic attribute of father,
many words might have been, and actually
were, formed, all equally fit to become, so
to say, the proper name of father.   In
Sanskrit protector can be expressed not
only by PA, followed by the derivative
suffix tar, but by pâ-la, pâ-laka, pâ-yú, all
meaning protector.   Now, the fact, that out
of many possible forms, *one* only has been
admitted into all the Aryan dictionaries,
shows that there must have been something
like a traditional usage in language long
before the separation of the Aryan family
took place.   Besides, there were other roots
from which the name of father might have
been formed, such as GAN, from which we
have *g*anitár, genitor, γενετήρ; or TAK, from
which the Greek τοκεύς; or PAR, from which
the Latin parens ; not to mention many

other names equally applicable to express some prominent attribute of a father in his relation to his children. If each Aryan dialect had formed its own name for father, from one of the many roots which all the Aryan dialects share in common, we should be able to say that there was a radical community between all these languages; but we should never succeed in proving— what is most essential—their historical community, or their divergence from one language which had already acquired a decided idiomatical consistency.

It happens, however, even with these, the most essential terms of an incipient civilisation, that one or the other of the Aryan dialects has lost the ancient expression, and replaced it by a new one. The common Aryan names for brother and sister, for instance, do not occur in Greek, where brother and sister are called ἀδελφός and ἀδελφή.[1] To conclude from this that at the time when the Greeks started from their Aryan home, the names of brother and sister had not yet been framed, would be a mistake. We have no reason to suppose that the Greeks were the first to leave, and, if we find that nations like the Teutonic or Celtic, who could have had no contact with the natives of India after the first separation had taken place, yet share the

[1] [Literally " co-uterine," born from the same womb, δελφύς.—Curtius, *Greek Etymology*, 5th ed., ii. 88.]

name of brother in common with Sanskrit, it is as certain that this name existed in the primitive Aryan language, as the occurrence of the same word in Wallachian and Portuguese would prove its Latin origin, though no trace of it existed in any of the other Romance-dialects. No doubt, the growth of language is governed by immutable laws, but the influence of accident is more considerable here than in any other branch of natural science ; and, though in this case it is possible to find a principle which determines the accidental loss [1] of the ancient names for brother and sister in Greek, yet this is not the case always, and we shall frequently find that one or the other Aryan dialect does not exhibit a term which yet, on the strength of our general argument, we shall feel justified in ascribing to the most ancient period of Aryan speech.

The mutual relation between brother and sister had been hallowed at that early period, and it had been sanctioned by names which had become traditional before the Aryan family broke up into different colonies. The original meaning of *bhrâtar* seems to have been he who carries or assists ; of *svasar*, she who pleases or consoles—*svasti* meaning in Sanskrit joy or happiness [literally " well-being " *su-asti*].

In duhitar, again, we find a name which must have become traditional long before

[1] See *Edinburgh Review*, Oct. 1851, p. 320.

the separation took place. It is a name identically the same in all the dialects, except Latin, and yet Sanskrit alone could have preserved a consciousness of its appellative power. Duhitar, as Professor Lassen has shown, is derived from DUH, a root, which in Sanskrit means, to milk. It is perhaps the Latin dūco, and the transition of meaning would be the same as between trahere, to draw, and traire, to milk. Now, the name of milkmaid, given to the daughter of the house, opens before our eyes a little idyll of the poetical and pastoral life of the early Aryans. One of the few things by which the daughter, before she was married, might make herself useful in a nomadic household, was the milking of the cattle, and it discloses a kind of delicacy and humour, even in the rudest state of society, if we imagine a father calling his daughter his little milkmaid, rather than *sutâ*, his begotten, or *filia*, the suckling.[1] This meaning, however, must have been forgotten long before the Aryans separated. Duhitar was then no longer a nickname, but it had become a technical term, or so to say, the proper name of daughter. That many words were formed in the same spirit, and

[1] [It is hardly likely that the Aryan parents had no word for their female offspring until she proved her usefulness in the dairy. The milk of which she was the 'drawer' (*duc-t(e)r-ix*) no doubt was that of her mother, not that of the cows. So 'daughter' is synonymous with *filia*, suckling.]

C

that they were applicable only during a nomadic state of life, we shall have frequent opportunity of seeing, as we go on. But as the transition of words of such special meaning into general terms, deprived of all etymological vitality, may seem strange, we may as well give at once a few analogous cases where, behind expressions of the most general currency, we can discover, by means of etymology, this peculiar background of the ancient nomad life of the Aryan nations. The very word *peculiar* may serve as an illustration taken from more modern times. Peculiar now means singular, extraordinary, but originally it meant what was private, *i.e.* not common, property ; being derived from peculium.[1]   Now, the Latin *peculium* stands for *pecudium* (like *consilium* for *considium*), and being derived from *pecus*, *pecudis*, it expressed originally what we should call cattle and chattle. Cattle constituting the chief personal property of agricultural people, we may well understand how peculiar, meaning originally what refers to one's own property, came to mean not-common, and at last, in our modern conversation, passed into the meaning of strange. I need hardly mention the well-known etymology of pecunia, which being

[1] [*Peculium*, 'lesser cattle,' meant the special possessions of the children of the household and of slaves (Mommsen, *History of Rome*, i. 194). So *chattles* is only another form of *cattle* (both from *capitalia*).]

derived from the same word, pecu, and therefore signifying flocks, took gradually the meaning of money, in the same manner as the Anglo-Saxon *feoh*, the German *Vieh*, cattle (and originally, according to Grimm's law, the same word as *pecu*), received in the course of time the sense of a pecuniary re-muneration, a fee.[1] What takes place in

[1] [Compare—

> Robin sat on the gude grene hill,
> Keipand a flock of *fie* [=sheep].
>
> R. Henryson, *Robin and Makyne*, ll. 1, 2.

> I ryde after this wyld *fee*.
>
> *Thomas of Erceldoune.*

On the other hand Old Eng. *aver* (Fr. *avoir*), "having," property, wealth, money, came to be used specifically for cattle, live stock, a farm beast (*N.E.D.*). Old Fris. *sket*, cattle (Old Slav. and Russ. *skotŭ*, cattle), is also used for coin (Goth. *skatts*, A.-Sax. *sceatt*, silver coin—H. M. Chadwick, *A.-Saxon Institutions*, p. 8). Possibly *herd*, cattle as a source of profit, O. H. Ger. *hërta*, pre-Teut. *kerdhâ*, is akin to Greek κέρδος, gain; just as 'gain' is akin to Old Fr. *gaaignier*, to feed flocks (M. Bréal, *Semantics*, 116), and Old Welsh *ysgrubl*, cattle, to *scribl* (=Lat. *scrupulum*), a coin, and Armor. *saout*, stock, to *solidus*, a coin (*id.* 117).

Heb. *kesītāh*, the silver which Jacob paid for a piece of ground (Gen. xxxiii. 19), was understood by the ancients to be a "lamb" (in value or impress). At all events Heb. *mikneh*, possession, wealth, is always used to signify cattle, like Ger. *gut*, just as Greek κτῆνος, cattle, is near akin to κτῆμα, possession. The Irish *bó-sluaiged*, riches, is from *bó-sluag, a herd of cows* (*sluag*, a host)—W. Stokes, *Irish Glosses*, 66; like *crodh*, (1) cattle, (2) money (Pictet, *Origines Indo-Européenes*, ii. 37, 337). It is different when coins are

modern languages, and, as it were, under our own eyes, must not surprise us in more distant ages. Now, the most useful cattle have always been the ox and the cow, and they seem to have constituted the chief riches and the most important means of subsistence among the Aryan nations. Ox and cow are called in Sanskrit *go*, plur. *gâvas*, which is the same word as the Old High German *chuo*, plur. *chuowi*, and with a change from the guttural to the labial media, the classical βοῦς, βόες, and *bôs*, *bôves*. The Slavonic languages also have preserved traces of this ancient name; for instance, the Lettish *gohws*, the Slavon. *govyado*, a herd, Serv. *govedar*, a cow-herd. From βοῦς we have in Greek βουκόλος, which meant originally a cow-herd, but in the verb βουκολέω, the meaning of tending cows has been absorbed by the more general one of tending cattle, nay, it is used in a metaphorical sense, such as ἐλπίσι βουκολοῦμαι, I feed myself on vain hopes. It is used with regard to horses, and thus we find for horse-herd, ἱππο-βούκολος, originally a cow-

called by the names of animals (from their impress), e.g. *mutton* of gold (see Cotgrave, *s.vv. mouton* and *vache*), Span. *ardita*, a coin, from Basque *ardia*, sheep (Diez).

Rupee, from the Hindustani *rûpiya*, silver, bullion, is traced to the Sanskrit *rûpa*, cattle. "In Homer, as in the early times of the Romans, in the Brehon Laws of Ireland, and the Vendidad of the Ancient Persians, value is estimated in cattle."—A. S. Wilkins (*Owens College Essays*, 315).]

herd of horses—an expression which we can only compare with Sanskrit *goyuga*, meaning a yoke of oxen, but afterwards any pair, so that a pair of oxen would be called *go-go-yuga*. Thus, in Sanskrit, *go-pa* means originally a cow-herd, but it soon loses this specific meaning, and is used for the head of a cow-pen, a herdsman, and at last, like the Greek ποιμὴν λαῶν, for a king.[1] From *gopa* a new verb is formed, *gopayati*, and in it all traces of its original meaning are obliterated ; it means simply to protect. As *gopa* meant a cow-herd, *go-tra*, in Sanskrit, was originally a hurdle, and meant the enclosure by which a herd was protected against thieves, and kept from straying. *Gotra*, however, has almost entirely lost its etymological power in the later Sanskrit, where the feminine only, *gotrā*, preserves the meaning of a herd of kine. In ancient times, when most wars were carried on, not to maintain the political equilibrium of Asia or Europe, but to take possession of good pasture, or to appropriate large herds of cattle,[2] the hurdles grew naturally into the walls of fortresses, the hedges became strongholds, and those who lived behind the same walls were called a *gotra*, a family, a tribe, a race. In

---

[1] [Similarly the Anglo-Indian *gaikwar*, *guicowar*, is etymologically a cow-herd (Mahratti, *gāekwar*, a king).]

[2] ὑπὲρ νομῆς ἢ λείας μαχόμεθα. *Toxar.* 36. Grimm, *Hist. of the German Language*, p. 17.

the *Veda*, *gotra* is still used in the sense
of folds or hurdles (iii. 39, 4)—

> Nákir [1] êshâm nindîtâ' mártyeshu
> Yé asmâ'kam pitárah góshu yodhâ'h
> I'ndrah eshâm drimhitâ' mâ'hinâvân
> Út gotrâ'ni sasrige damsánâvân.

'Not is there among men one scoffing at
them who were our fathers, who fought among
the cows. Indra, the mighty, is their defender ;
he, the powerful, spread out their hurdles,[2] *i.e.*
their possessions.'

'Fighting among or for the cows,' *goshu-
yúdh*, is used in the *Veda* as a name for
warrior, in general, i. 112, 22, and one of
the most frequent words for battle is
gáv-ishti, literally 'striving for cows.' In
the later Sanskrit, however, *gaveshana*
means simply, research (physical or philosophical), *gavesh*, to inquire. Again, *goshtha*
means cow-pen or stable ($\beta o \acute{v} \sigma \tau a \theta \mu o \nu$), but,
with the progress of time and civilisation
goshthî became the name of an assembly,
nay, it was used to express discussion and
gossip, as gossip also meant originally a
godfather or godmother, and then took the

---

[1] [In later editions corrected to Nákih.]

[2] Hurdle seems to be the Vaidik *Khardis*, house,
i.e. enclosure, and from the same root we have Anglo-
Saxon *heord*, a herd, and old Norse *hirdr*, bene custo-
ditus. Perhaps Latin *cors*, *cortis* (*cohors*, *cohortis*)
comes from the same source, meaning an enclosed
ground, a court, and at last a palace. [*Hurdle*, quite
distinct from *herd*, like Ger. *hürde*, is akin to Greek
$\kappa \acute{v} \rho \tau o s$, cage, from Sansk. root *kart*, to interweave—
Kluge. *Cors* is unconnected.]

abstract sense of idle conversation or tattle.[1]

All these words, composed with *go*, cattle, to which many more might have been added if we were not afraid of trying the patience of our less [more ?] sceptical readers, prove that the people who formed them must have led a half nomadic and pastoral life, and we may well understand how the same people came to use duhitar in the sense of daughter. Language has been called a map of the science and manners of the people who speak it, and we should probably find, if we examined the language of a maritime people, that instead of cattle and pasture, ships and water would form part of many words which afterwards took a more general meaning.

We proceed to examine other terms which indicate the state of society previous to the separation of the Aryan race, and which we hope will give to our distant picture that expression of truth and reality which can be appreciated even by those who have never seen the original.

We pass over the words for son, partly because their etymology is of no interest, their meaning being simply that of natus, born,[2]

1 [It is curious to note the English dialect and Anglo-Irish *goster*, to prate, tattle, or gossip, Irish *gastaire*, a prater, *goistigh*, a gossip, a god-parent, as corresponding in form and meaning.]

2 For instance,—Sk. *sûnú*, Goth. *sunus*, Lith. *sunus*, all from *su*, to beget, whence Greek υἱός, but by a

partly because the position of the son, or the successor and inheritor of his father's wealth and power, would claim a name at a much earlier time than daughter, sister, or brother. All these relations in fact, expressed by *father* and *mother*, *son* and *daughter*, *brother* and *sister*, are fixed, we should say, by the laws of nature, and their acknowledgment in language would not prove any considerable advance in civilisation, however appropriately the names themselves might have been chosen. But there are other relations, of later origin, and of a more conventional character, sanctioned, it is true, by the laws of society, but not proclaimed by the voice of nature —relations which are aptly expressed in English by the addition of in-law, as father-in-law, mother, son, daughter, brother and sister-in-law. If the names for these relations could be vindicated for the earliest period of Aryan civilisation, we should have gained something considerable, for though there is hardly a dialect in Africa or Australia in which we do not find words for father, mother, son, daughter, brother, and sister, and hardly a tribe in which these natural degrees of relationship are not

---

different suffix. Sansk. *putra*, son, is of doubtful origin, but probably of considerable antiquity, as it is shared by the Celtic branch (Bret. *paotr)*. The Lat. *puer* is supposed to be derived from the same root. [These latter words are probably from the Sanskrit root *pu*, to beget—Curtius, *Greek Etymology*, 3rd ed., i. 345.]

hallowed, there are languages in which the degrees of affinity have never received expression, and tribes who ignore their very meaning.

	Sanskrit.	Greek.	Latin.	Gothic.	Slav.	Celtic.
Father-in-law:	svásura	ἑκυρός	socer	svaíhra	svekr	chwegrwn
Mother-in-law:	svasrû́	ἑκυρά	socrus	svaíhro	svekry	W. chwegyr
Son-in-law:	gâ'mâtar	γαμβρός	gener	...	...	...
Daughter-in-law:	snushâ	νυός	nurus	snûr	snocha	...
Brother-in-law:	dêvár' (ανδράδελφος) (nânandar)	δαήρ / γάλως (ανδραδελφη)	levir glos	tâcor	deweris (Lith.)...	...
Sister-in-law:	yâtaras (wives of brothers) syâlá (wife's brother) syâlî (wife's sister)	εἰνάτερες / αέλιοι and / εἰλιόνες (husbands of sisters)	janitrices	...	jatrew (Pol.)	...

The above table shows that, before the

separation of the Aryan race, every one of the degrees of affinity had received expression and sanction in language ; for although some spaces had to be left empty, the coincidences, such as they are, are sufficient to warrant one general conclusion. If we find in Sanskrit the word putra, son, and in Celtic, again, paotr, son, root and suffix being the same, we must remember that, although none of the other Aryan dialects has preserved this word in exactly the same form, yet the identity of the Celtic and Sanskrit term can only be explained on the supposition that putra was a common Aryan term, well known before any branch of this family was severed from the common stem.

In modern languages we might, if dealing with similar cases, feel inclined to admit a later communication, but fortunately, in ancient languages, no such intercourse was possible, after the southern branch of the Aryan family had once crossed the Himâlaya, and the northern branch set foot on the shores of Europe. Different questions are raised where, as is the case with gâmâtar and γαμβρós, originally bridegroom or husband,[1] then son-in-law, we are only able to prove that the same root was taken, and therefore the same radical idea expressed by Greek and Sanskrit, while the derivation is

[1] Ταμβρòς καλεῖται ὁ γήμας ὑπὸ τῶν οἰκείων τῆς γαμηθείσης.

peculiar in each language. Here no doubt we must be more careful in our conclusions, but generally, we shall find that these formal differences are only such as occur in dialects of the same language, when out of many possible forms, used at first promiscuously, one was chosen by one poet, one by another, and then became popular and traditional. This at least is more likely than to suppose that to express a relation which might be expressed in such various ways, the Greek should have chosen the same root γαμ to form γαμρὸς and γαμβρός, independently of the Hindu, who took the same root for the same purpose, only giving it a casual form (as in bhrâtar instead of bhartar), and appending to it the usual suffix, tar ; thus forming gâ'mâ-tar, instead of gamara or yamara. Again, when it happens that one of these languages has lost a common term, we are sometimes enabled to prove its former existence by means of derivatives. In Greek, for instance, at least in the literary language, there is no trace of nepos, grandson, which we have in Sanskrit nápât, Germ. nefo ; nor of neptis, Sk. naptî, Germ. nift. Yet there is in Greek ἀ-νεψιός, a first-cousin, *i.e.* one with whom we are grandsons together, as the uncle is called the little-grandfather, avunculus, from avus. This word ἀνεψιός is formed like Latin consobrinus, *i.e.* consororinus, one with whom we are sister-children, our modern cousin, It. cugino, in which there remains very little of the word soror, from which however it is derived. 'A-νεψιός therefore proves that in Greek also, νεπους must have existed in the sense of child or grandchild, and it is by a similar process that we can prove the former presence in Greek of a term corresponding to Sk. syâla, a wife's brother. In Sanskrit a husband calls his wife's brother syâla, his wife's sister syâlî. Therefore in Greek Peleus would call Amphitrite, and Poseidon Thetis, their syâlîs : having married sisters, they would have syâlîs in common—they would be what the Greeks call ἀ-έλιοι, for sy between two vowels is generally dropped in Greek ; and the only anomaly consists in the short ε representing the long â in Sanskrit.

There are still a few words which throw a dim light on the early organisation of the Aryan family life. The position of the widow was acknowledged in language and in law, and we find no trace that, at that early period, she who had lost her husband was doomed to die with him. If this custom had existed, the want of having a name for widow would hardly have been felt, or, if it had been, the word would most likely have had some reference to this awful rite. Now, husband, or man, in Sanskrit is dhava, a word which does not seem to exist in the other Aryan languages, except perhaps in

Celtic, where Pictet brings forward the analogous form, dea, a man or person. From dhava, Sanskrit forms the name of the widow by the addition of the preposition vi, which means without; therefore vidhavâ, husbandless, widow.[1] This compound has been preserved in languages which have lost the simple word dhava, thus showing the great antiquity of this traditional term. We have it not only in Celtic feadbh, but in Gothic viduvo, Slav. v[i]dova, Old Prussian widdewû, and Latin vidua. If the custom of widow-burning had existed at that early period, there would have been no vidhavâs, no husbandless women, because they would all have followed their husband into death. Therefore the very name indicates what we are further enabled to prove by historical evidence, the late origin of widow-burning in India. It is true, that when the English Government prohibited this melancholy custom, and when the whole of India seemed on the verge of a religious revolution, the Brahmans appealed to the *Veda* as the authority for this sacred rite, and as they had the promise that their religious practices should not be interfered with, they claimed respect for the Suttee. They actually quoted chapter and

[1] [Later Sanskritists prefer to deduce the word from the Vedic root *vidh*, to be empty (bereaved)—Curtius, i. 40, whence Lat. *di-vid-ere.* So the widow would be one *void*, *de-void* of a mate, or *di-vided* from him, Lat. *vidua.*]

verse from the *Rigveda*, and Colebrooke,[1] the most accurate and learned Sanskrit scholar we have ever had, has translated this passage in accordance with their views :

'Om! let these women, not to be widowed, good wives adorned with collyrium, holding clarified butter, consign themselves to the fire! Immortal, not childless, not husbandless, well adorned with gems, let them pass into the fire, whose original element is water.' (From the *Rigveda*.)

Now this is perhaps the most flagrant instance of what can be done by an unscrupulous priesthood. Here have thousands and thousands of lives been sacrificed and a fanatical rebellion been threatened on the authority of a passage which was mangled, mistranslated, and misapplied. If anybody had been able at the time to verify this verse of the *Rigveda*, the Brahmans might have been beaten with their own weapons ; nay, their spiritual prestige might have been considerably shaken. The *Rigveda*, which now hardly one Brahman out of a hundred is able to read, so far from enforcing the burning of widows, shows clearly that this custom was not sanctioned during the earliest period of Indian history. According to the hymns of the *Rigveda* and the Vaidik ceremonial, contained in the Grihyasûtras, the wife accompanies the corpse of her husband to the funeral pile,

[1] On the Duties of a Faithful Widow, *Asiatic Researches*, vol. iv. pp. 209, 219.   Calcutta, 1795.

but she is there addressed with a verse taken from the *Rigveda*, and ordered to leave her husband, and to return to the world of the living.[1] 'Rise up, woman,' it is said, 'come to the world of life; thou sleepest nigh unto him whose life is gone. Come to us. Thou hast thus fulfilled thy duties of a wife to the husband who once took thy hand, and made thee mother.'

This verse is preceded by the very verse which the later Brahmans have falsified and quoted in support of their cruel tenet. The reading of the verse is beyond all doubt, for there is no various reading, in our sense of the word, in the whole of the *Rigveda*. Besides, we have the commentaries and the ceremonials, and nowhere is there any difference as to the text or its meaning. It is addressed to the other women who are present at the funeral, and who have to pour oil and butter on the pile.

'May these women who are not widows, but have good husbands, draw near with oil and butter. Those who are mothers may go up first to the altar, without tears, without sorrow, but decked with fine jewels.'

---

[1] See Grimm's Essay on *The Burning of the Dead;* Roth's article on *The Burial in India;* Professor Wilson's article on *The supposed Vaidik authority for the burning of Hindu Widows*, and my own translation of the complete documentary evidence in the *Journal of the German Oriental Society*, vol. ix. fasc. 4. Professor Wilson was the first to point out the falsification of the text, and the change of 'yonim agre' into 'yonim agne*h*.' [See also H. J. Bushby, *Widow Burning*, 1855.]

Now the words ' the mothers may go first to the altar,' are in Sanskrit.

' Â rohantu *g*anayo yonim agre ; '

and this the Brahmans have changed into

' Â rohantu *g*anayo yonim agne*h* ; '

—a small change, but sufficient to consign many lives to the womb (yonim) of fire (agne*h*).[1]

After this digression, we return to the earlier period of history of which language alone can give us any information, and, as we have claimed for it the name of widow, or the husbandless, we need not wonder that the name of husband also is the same to this day in most of the Aryan languages, which had been fixed upon by the Aryans before their separation. It is pati in Sanskrit, meaning originally strong, like Latin potis or potens. In Lithuanian the form is exactly the same, patis, and this, if we apply Grimm's law, becomes faths in Gothic.

---

[1] In a similar manner the custom of widow-burning has been introduced by the Brahmans in an interpolated passage of the *Toy-Cart*, an Indian drama of King Sudraka, which was translated by Prof. Wilson, and has lately been performed at Paris. *Le Chariot d'Enfant*, Drame en vers en cinq actes et sept tableaux, traduction du Drame Indien du Roi Soudraka, par MM. Méry et Gerard de Nerval. Paris, 1850. [See Goldstücker, *Literary Remains*, i. 199–202; M. Müller, *Anthropological Religion*, 259; compare a similarly fatal blunder causing countless immolations due to a misunderstanding of the name Jagan-nāth (T. W. R. Davids, *Hibbert Lectures*, 33.]

In Greek, again, we find πόσις instead of πότις. Now, the feminine of pati in Sanskrit is patnî, and there is no doubt that the Old Prussian pattin, in the accusative waispattin, and the Greek πότνια, are mere transcripts of it, all meaning the mistress.

What the husband was in his house—the lord, the strong protector—the king was among his people. Now, a common name for people was vis in Sanskrit, from which the title of the third caste, the householders, or Vaisyas, is derived. It comes from the same root from which we have in Sanskrit vesa, house, οἶκος, vicus, Goth. veihs, German wich, and the modern English termination of many names of places. Hence vispati in Sanskrit meant king, *i.e.* lord of the people, and that this compound had become a title sanctioned by Aryan etiquette before the separation, is confirmed in a strange manner by the Lithuanian wiêsz-patis, a lord, wiesz-patene, a lady, as compared with the Sanskrit vis-patis and -patnî. There was therefore, at that early period, not only a nicely-organised family life, but the family began to become absorbed by the state, and here again conventional titles had been fixed, and were handed down perhaps two thousand years before the title of Cæsar was heard of.

Another name for people being dâsa or dasyu, dâsa-pati no doubt was an ancient name for king. There is, however, this great difference between vis and dâsa, that the former means people, the latter subjects, conquered races, nay originally, enemies.[1] Dasyu in the *Veda* is enemy, but in the *Zendavesta*, where we have the same word, it means provinces or gentes ; and Darius calls himself, in his Mountain-records, ' King of Persia and King of the provinces ' (Kshâya-thîya Pârsaiya, Kshâyathîya dahyunâm). Hence it is hardly doubtful that the Greek δεσ-πότης represents a Sanskrit title dâsa pati, lord of nations,[2] but we cannot admit that the title of Hospodar, which has lately become so notorious, should, as Bopp says, be the same as Sanskrit vispati, or as dâsapati. The word is gaspadorus in Lithuanian ; in Old Slav. gospod, gospodin, and gospodar ; Pol. gospodarz ; Boh. hospodár. A Slavonic g, however, does not correspond to Sanskrit w or d, nor could the t of pati become d.[3] Benfey, who derives gospod from the Vaidik gaspati, avoids the former, but not the latter difficulty, and it is certainly better to state these difficulties than to endeavour to smuggle in some ancient Aryan terms, in defiance of laws which can never be violated with impunity.

[1] [Sanskrit *dasa-s*, slave, bondman, akin to Greek δε-ω, to bind—Curtius, i. 279.]

[2] [Elsewhere M. Müller prefers to equate δέσ-ποτης with the Sansk. *dám-pati*, for *dams-pati* (=*domûs-potens*), ' house-master.' See *Chips*, 1907, iv. 256.]

[3] See Schleicher's excellent remarks in his *Formenlehre der Kirchenslawischen Sprache*, 1852, p. 107.

A third common Aryan word for king is râg, in the *Veda ;* rex, regis, in Latin ; reiks in Gothic, a word still used in German, as reich, regnum, Frank-reich, regnum Francorum ; and Irish riogh ; Welsh ri.

A fourth name for king and queen is simply father and mother. Ganaka in Sanskrit means father, from GAN, to beget ; it also occurs, as the name of a well-known king, in the *Veda.* This is the Old German chuning, the English king.[1] Mother in Sanskrit is ganí, the Greek γυνή, the Gothic qinô, the Slav. zena, the English queen.[2] *Queen,* therefore, means originally mother, or lady ; and thus again we see how the language of the family life grew gradually into the political language of the oldest Aryan state, and how the brotherhood of the family became the φρατρια of the state.

We have seen that the name of house was known before the Aryan family broke up towards the south and the north, and we might bring further evidence to this effect by comparing Sk. dama, with Greek δόμος, Lat. domus, Slav. domŭ, Celt. daimh, and Goth. timrjan, to build, from which

---

[1] [King is related to the Sanskrit word rather than directly descended from it. It is shortened from *kining* (A.-Sax. *cyn-ing*), 'son of the kin' or (royal) family, a prince—H. M. Chadwick, *A.-Sax. Institutions,* 302. But *kin,* A.-Sax. *cynn,* is from *gan,* to beget.]

[2] [*Queen,* A.-Sax. *cwēn,* Goth. *kwēns,* a woman, distinct from *quean,* is not from the same root as *king* (Skeat, *Notes on Eng. Etymology,* 235).]

English timber, though we doubt the identity of the Slavonic grod and gorod, the Lithuanian grod, with the Gothic gards, Lat. hort-us, Greek χόρτος, all meaning an enclosed ground.[1] The most essential part of a house, particularly in ancient times, being a door well fastened and able to resist the attacks of enemies ; we are glad to find the ancient name preserved in Sanskrit, dvar, dvâras, Goth. daur, Lith. durrys, Celt. dor, Greek θύρα, Lat. fores. The builder also, or architect, has the same name in Sanskrit and Greek, takshan being the Greek τέκτων. The Greek ἄστυ, again, has been compared with Sk. vâstu, house ; the Greek κώμη, with Gothic haims, a village : the English home. Still more conclusive as to the early existence of cities, is the Sk. puri, town, preserved by the Greeks in their name for town, πόλις ; and that high-roads also were not unknown, appears from Sanskrit path, pathi, panthan, and pâthas, all names for path, the Greek πάτος, the Gothic fad, which Bopp believes to be identical with Lat. pons, pontis, and Slav. ponti.

It would take a volume were we to examine all the relics of language, though, no doubt, every new word would strengthen our argument, and add, as it were, a new stone from which this ancient and venerable ruin of the Aryan mind might be reconstructed. The evidence, however, which we

[1] [Curtius (i. 235) admits the relationship.]

have gone through must be sufficient to show that the race of men which could coin these words—words that have been carried down the stream of time, and washed up on the shores of so many nations—could not have been a race of savages, of mere nomads and hunters. Nay, it should be observed, that most of the terms connected with chase and warfare differ in each of the Aryan dialects, while words connected with more peaceful occupations, belong generally to the common heirloom of the Aryan language. The proper appreciation of this fact in its general bearing will show how a similar remark made by Niebuhr with regard to Greek and Latin, requires a very different explanation from that which that great scholar, from his more restricted point of view, was able to give it. It will show that all the Aryan nations had led a long life of peace before they separated, and that their language acquired individuality and nationality, as each colony started in search of new homes—new generations forming new terms connected with the warlike and adventurous life of their onward migrations. Hence it is that not only Greek and Latin, but all Aryan languages have their peaceful words in common; and hence it is that they all differ so strangely in their warlike expressions. Thus the domestic animals are generally known by the same name in England and in India, while the wild beasts have different names, even in Greek and Latin. I can only give a list (p. 55), which must tell its own story, for it would take too much time to enter into the etymological formation of all these words, though no doubt a proper understanding of their radical meaning would make them more instructive as living witnesses to the world of thought and the primitive household of the Aryan race.

Of wild animals some were known to the Aryans before they separated, and they happen to be animals which live both in Asia and Europe, the bear and the wolf.

	Sanskrit.	Greek.	Italian.	Teutonic.	Slavonic.
Bear :	ŕiksha	ἄρκτος	ursus		
Wolf :	vŕika	λύκος	{ lupus (v)irpus }	vulfs	wilka

To them should be added the serpent.

Serpent :	{ ahi	sarpa }	{ ἔχις (ἔγχελυς) ἕρπετον }	{ anguis (anguilla) serpens }	ungury	R. ûgorj

Without dwelling on the various names of those animals which had partly been tamed and domesticated, while others were then, as they are now, the natural enemies of the shepherd and his flocks, we proceed at once to mention a few words which indicate that this early pastoral life was not without some of the most primitive arts, such as ploughing, grinding, weaving, and the working of precious and useful metals.

The oldest term for ploughing is AR, which we find in Lat. arare, Greek ἀροῦν,

	Sanskrit and Zend.	Greek.	Italian.	Teutonic.	Lithuanian.	Slav.	Celtic.
Cattle:	pasu / paçu	πῶυ	pecu	G. faihu / O.H.G. fihu	Pruss. pecku	...	...
Ox and cow:	go (nom. gaus) / gâo	βοῦς	bos	O.H.G. chuo	Lett. gohw	Slav. govjado	...
Ox:	ukshan (ukhshan / vakhsha)	...	vacca ?	G. auhsan	...	...	W. ych
Steer:	sthûrâ / stavra	ταῦρος	taurus	stiur	...	tour	[Ir. *tarbh*]
Heifer:	stari	στεῖρα	(sterilis)	stairo	...	...	...
Horse:	âçu, asva / açpa	ἵππος	equus	G. aihus	aszwa	...	W. osw
Foal:	...	πῶλος	pullus	G. fula	...	...	...
Dog:	svan (spâ, σπάκα)	κύων	canis	O.H.G. hund	szu	R. sobaka / Bulg. kuce	G. cu
Sheep:	avi	ὄϊς	ovis	G. avi-str / E. ewe	awi	Slav. ovjza	...
Calf:	vatsa	ἴταλος	vitulus	...	...	...	...
He-goat:	ajâ / açâ	κάπρος	caper	O.H.G. hafr	...	...	[Gr. *gábhar*] / G. aighe
She-goat:	...	αἴξ	...	...	ozis	...	...
Sow:	sû (kara)	ὗς	sus	O.H.G. sû	...	svinia	[Ir. (*p*)*orc*]
Pig:	prishat	πόρκος	porcus	O.H.G. farah	parszas	Pol. prosie	...
Hog:	grishvi	χοῖρος	...	O.N. grís	...	...	...
Donkey:	...	ὄνος	asinus	asilo	...	...	...
Mouse:	mûsh	μῦς	mus	O.H.G. mûs	musse	Pol. mysz	...
Fly:	makshikâ	μυῖα	musca	O.H.G. micco	...	R. mucha	...
Goose:	hansa	χήν	anser	O.H.S. kans	zasis	Boh. hus	G. ganra

Old High German aran, to ear, Russ. orati, Lithuanian arti, and Gaelic ar. From this verb we have the common name of the plough, ἄροτρον, aratrum, Old Saxon erida, Old Norse ardhr, Slavonic oralo and oradlo, Lith. arimnas, and Corn. aradar. Ἄρουρα and arvum come probably from the same root. But a more general name for field is Sk. pada, Greek πέδον, Umbrian perum, Pol. pole,[1] Saxon folda, O.H.G. feld, field ; or ἀγρός, ager, and Goth. akrs.

The corn which was grown in Asia could not well have been the same which the Aryan nations afterwards cultivated in more northern regions. Some of the names, however, have been preserved, and may be supposed to have had, if not exactly the same, at least a similar botanical character. Such are Sk. yava, Zend. yava, Lithuanian jawas, which in Greek must be changed to ζέα. Sk. sveta means white, and corresponds to Gothic hveit, O.H.G. huiz, and wiz, the Anglo-Saxon hvît, and Lithuanian kwêtys. But the name of the colour became also the name of the white grain,[2]

---

[1] [This and the words following are not connected with those preceding.]

[2] [Compare Welsh *gwenith*, wheat, and *gwen*, white ; and It. *scandella*, Span. Portg. *escandia*, a kind of wheat, probably from Lat. *candidus*, white (Diez) ; ἄλφι, ἄλφιτον, barley meal, from ἀλφός (*albus*), white ; Old Fr. *blanc*, white wheat (Cotgrave), opposed to *nielle*, nigella, cockle ; Pers. *chîd*, wheat, connected by Pictet with Sansk. *çvind*, to be white. Ir. *cruith-neacht*, wheat, is the ' red.']

and thus we have Gothic hvaitei, Lith. kwec'io, the English wheat, with which some scholars have compared the Slav, shito, and the Greek σῖτος. The name of corn signified originally what is crushed or ground. Thus *Kurna* in Sanskrit means ground, and from the same radical element we must no doubt derive the Russian zerno, the Goth. kaurn, the Latin granum. In Lithuanian, girna is a mill-stone, and the plural girnôs is the name of a hand-mill. The Russian word for mill-stone is, again, shernov, and the Gothic name for mill, qvairnus, the later quirn. The English name for mill is likewise of considerable antiquity, for it exists not only in the O.H.G. muli, but in the Lithuanian malunas, the Bohemian mlyn, the Welsh melin, the Latin mola, and the Greek μύλη.

We might add the names for cooking and baking, and the early distinction between flesh and meat, to show that the same aversion which is expressed in later times, for instance, by the poets of the *Veda*, against tribes eating raw flesh, was felt already during this primitive period.

Kravya-ad (κρέας-έδω) and âma-ad (ὠμός-έδω) are names applied to barbarians, and used with the same horror in India as ὠμοφάγοι[1] and κρεωφάγοι in Greece. But we can only now touch on these points, and must leave

---

[1] [The Eskimo (Ayeskimeou) were so named by the Indians as 'raw-eaters.' But see Payne, *New World*, ii. 350.]

it to another opportunity to bring out in full relief this old picture of human life.[1]

As the name for clothes is the same among all the Aryan nations, being vastra in Sanskrit, vasti in Gothic, vestis in Latin, ἐσθής in Greek, gwisk in Celtic, we are justified in ascribing to the Aryan ancestors the art of weaving as well as of sowing. To weave in Sanskrit is ve, and, in a causative form, vap. With ve coincide the Latin vieo, and the Greek radical in Ϝή-τριον; with vap, the O.H.G. wab, the Engiish weave, the Greek ὑφ-αίνω.

To sew, in Sanskrit, is siv, from which sûtra, a thread. The same root is preserved in Latin suo, in Gothic siuja, in O.H.G. siwu, the English to sew, Lithuanian suwú, Slav. shivu, Greek κασσύω for κατασύω. Another Sanskrit root, with a very similar meaning, is NAH, which must have existed also as nabh and nadh. From nah we have Latin neo and necto, Greek νέω, German nâhan, and nâvan, to sew; from nadh, the Greek νήθω; from nabh, the Sanskrit nâbhi, and nâbha or ûrnanâbha, the spider, literally the wool-spinner.[2]

There is a fourth root which seems to

[1] [For a full treatment of the subject see Adolphe Pictet, *Les Origines Indo-Européenes, ou les Aryas Primitifs, Essai de Paleontologie Linguistiques*, 2 tom., and O. Schrader, *Prehistoric Antiquities of the Aryan Peoples* (trans. Jevons), 1890.]

[2] [Compare *wevet* (weaver, weft), a Wessex word for a spider and its web. *Spider* itself is *spinder*, the ' spinner.']

have had originally the special meaning of sewing or weaving, but which afterwards took in Sanskrit the more general sense of making. This is ra*k*, which may correspond to the Greek ῥάπτω, to stitch together, or to weave ; nay, which might account for another name of the spider, ἀράχνη in Greek, and aranea in Latin, and for the classical name of woven wool, λάχνος or λάχνη, and the Latin lana.

That the value and usefulness of some of the metals was known before the separation of the Aryan race, can be proved only by a few words ; for the names of most of the metals differ in different countries.[1] Yet there can be no doubt that iron was known, and its value appreciated, whether for defence or for attack. Whatever its old Aryan name may have been, it is clear that Sanskrit ayas, Latin ahes in aheneus, and even the contracted form aes, aeris, the Gothic ais, the Old High German er, and the English iron, are names cast in the same mould, and only slightly corroded even now by the rust of so many centuries. The names of the precious metals, such as gold and silver, have suffered more in passing through the hands of so many generations. But, notwithstanding, we are able to discover even in the Celtic airgiod the traces of the Sanskrit ra*g*ata, the Greek ἄργυρος, the Latin argentum ; and even in the

[1] [See N. Joly, *Man before Metals*, 1883.]

Gothic gulth, gold, a similarity has been detected with the Slavonic zlato and Russian zoloto, Greek χρύσος and Sanskrit hiraɴyam, only that the terminations differ widely. The radical seems to have been harat, from whence the Sanskrit harit, the colour of the sun and of the dawn, as aurum also descends from the same root with aurora. Some of the iron implements used, whether for peaceful or warlike purposes, have kept their original name, and it is curious to find the exact similarity of the Sanskrit paraѕu, and the Greek πέλεκυς, axe, or of Sanskrit asi, sword, and Latin ensis.

New ideas do not gain ground at once, and there is a tendency in our mind to resist new convictions as long as we can. Hence it is only by a gradual and careful accumulation of facts that we can hope to establish on this linguistic evidence the reality of a period in the history of mankind previous to the beginning of the most ancient known dialects of the Aryan world —previous to the origin of Sanskrit as well as Greek—previous to the time when the first Greek arrived on the shores of Asia Minor, and looking at the vast expanse of sea and country to the west and north, called it *Europa*. Let us examine one other witness, whose negative evidence will be important. During this early period the ancestors of the Aryan race must have occupied a more central position in Asia, whence the southern branches extended towards India, the northern to Asia Minor and Europe. It would follow, therefore, that before their separation, they could not have known the existence of the sea, and hence, if our theory be true, the name for sea must be of later growth, and different in the Aryan languages. And this expectation is fully confirmed. We find, indeed, identical names in Greek and Latin, but not in the northern and southern branches of the Aryan family. And even these Greek and Latin names are evidently metaphorical expressions—names that existed in the ancient language, and were transferred to this new phenomenon. Pontus and πόντος mean sea in the same sense as Homer speaks of ὑγρὰ κέλευθα, for pontus comes from the same source from which we have pons, pontis, and the Sanskrit pantha, if not pâthas. The sea was not called a barrier, but a high-road—more useful for trade and travel than any other road—and Prof. Curtius [1] has well pointed out Greek expressions, such as πόντος ἁλὸς πολιῆς, and θάλασσα πόντου, as indicating, even among the Greeks, a consciousness of the original import of πόντος. Nor can words like Sanskrit salila, Latin sal, and Greek ἅλς, ἁλός, be quoted as proving an acquaintance

[1] See Kuhn's *Journal of Comparative Philology*, i. 34. Prof. Curtius gives the equation : πόντος : πάτος = πένθος : πάθος = βένθος : βάθος.

with the sea among the early Aryans.
They may have known the use of salt, but
this is all that could be proved by ἅλς, sal,
and salila ; the application of these words
to the sea belongs to later times. The
same remark applies to words like aequor in
Latin, or πέλαγος in Greek. Θάλασσα has
long been proved to be a dialectical form of
θάρασσα or τάρασσα, expressing the troubled
waves of the sea (ἐτάραξε δὲ πόντον Ποσειδῶν),
and if the Latin mare be the same as
Sanskrit vâri, vâri in Sanskrit does not
mean sea, but water in general, and could,
therefore, only confirm the fact that all the
Aryan nations applied terms of a general
meaning when they had each to fix their
names for the sea. But mare is more likely
a name for dead or stagnant water, like
Sanskrit maru, the desert, derived from
mri, to die ; and though it is identical with
Gothic marei, Slav. more, Irish muir, the
application of all these words to the ocean
is of later date.[1] But, although the sea
had not yet been reached by the Aryan
nations before their common language
branched off into various dialects, naviga-
tion was well known to them. The words
oar and rudder can be traced back to
Sanskrit, and the name of the ship is

[1] [Moor is probably the dead barren land akin to
Pers. meru, desert, Sansk. and Zend. mara, death ;
see Geiger, Development of the Human Race, 154;
C. F. Keary, Primitive Belief, 276. Cf. Icel. blá-mœr,
'blue moor,' the sea—Vigfusson, 67.]

identically the same in Sanskrit (naus, nâvas), in Latin (navis), in Greek (ναῦς), and in Teutonic (Old High German nacho, A.S. naca.) [A.-Sax. *snacc*, a 'smack '].

It is hardly possible to look at the evidence hitherto collected, and which, if space allowed, might have been considerably increased,[1] without feeling that these words are the fragments of a real language, once spoken by a united race at a time which the historian has till lately hardly ventured to realise, except on the authority of the sacred writings of the Jews. Yet here we have in our own hands, the relics of that distant time ; we are using the same words which were used by the fathers of the Aryan race, changed only by phonetic influences ; nay, we are as near to them in thought and speech as the French and Italians are to the ancient people of Rome. If any more proof was wanted as to the reality of that period which must have preceded the dispersion of the Aryan race, we might appeal to the Aryan numerals, as irrefragable evidence of that long-continued intellectual life which characterises that period. Here is a decimal system of numeration, perhaps one of the

---

[1] A large collection of common Aryan words is found in Grimm's History of the German Language. The first attempt to use them for historical purposes was made by Eichhof; but the most useful contributions have since been made by Winning in his *Manual of Comparative Philology*, 1838 ; by Kuhn, Curtius, and Förstemann ; and much new material is to be found in Bopp's *Glossary* and Pott's *Etymologische Forschungen.*

most marvellous achievements of the human mind, based on an abstract conception of quantity, regulated by a spirit of philosophical classification, and yet conceived, matured, and finished before the soil of Europe was trodden by Greek, Roman, Slave, or Teuton. Such a system could only have been formed by a very small community, and more than any part of language it seems to necessitate the admission of conventional agreement among those who first framed and adopted the Aryan names for one to hundred. Let us imagine as well as we can, that at the present moment, we were suddenly called upon to invent new names for one, two, three, and we may then begin to feel what kind of task it was to form and fix these names. We could easily supply new expressions for material objects, because they always have some attributes which language can render either metaphorically or periphrastically. We could call the sea the salt water, the rain, the water of heaven, the rivers, the daughters of the earth. Numbers, however, are, by their very nature, such abstract and empty conceptions, that it tries our ingenuity to the utmost to find any attributive element in them to which expression might be given, and which might in time become the proper name of a merely quantitative idea.[1]   There

[1] [Prof. Goldstücker attempted to analyse the numerals etymologically as follows in the Sanskrit :

might be less difficulty for one and two ;
and hence, these two numerals have received
more than one name in the Aryan family.
But this again would only create a new
difficulty, because, if different people were
allowed to use different names for the same
numeral, the very object of these names
would be defeated. If five could be expressed by a term meaning the open hand,
and might also be rendered by the simple
plural of fingers, these two synonymous
terms would be useless for the purpose of
any exchange of thought. Again, if a word
meaning fingers or toes might have been
used to express five as well as ten, all com-
merce between individuals using the same
word in different senses, would have been
rendered impossible. Hence, in order to
form and fix a series of words expressing one,

one='he'; two='diversity'; three='what-goes-be-
yond'; four=(one) 'and-three'; five='coming after';
six=(two and) 'four'; seven='following'; eight=
'two-fours'; nine='what-comes-after' (*nava*, new);
ten='two-and-eight.' See also W. H. Ferrar, *Comparative Grammar of Sanskrit, Greek, and Latin*,
306–309.

The Assyrian numerals have tentatively been in-
terpreted thus : 1, *khad*, 'the hand'; 2, *sin*, 'repetition,' 'double'; 3, *salas*, '(what comes) after'; 4,
arbā (*rabā*), 'increased,' 'multiplied'; 5, *khames*, 'the
fist'; 6, *sis*, 'the other (hand)'; 7, *siba*, 'great (extended) six'; 8, *sam-na*, 'six-and-two'; 9, *ti-si(t)*,
'ten less one'; 10, *esru*, 'united (hands).'—Bertin,
Trans. Bib. Archæolog. Soc., vol. vii. pp. 370 *seq.*
Much speculative matter will be found in R. Ellis,
Numerals as Signs of Primeval Unity among Mankind,
1873. See also G. Hempl, *Classical Review*, Nov.
1902.]

E

two, three, four, &c., it was necessary that the ancestors of the Aryan race should have come to a formal agreement to use but one term for each number, and to attach but one meaning to each term. This was not the case with regard to other words, as may be seen by the large proportion of synonymous and polyonymous terms by which every ancient language is characterised— the wear and tear of language in literary and practical usage being alone able to reduce the exuberance of this early growth, and to give to each object but one name, and to each name but one power. And all this must have been achieved with regard to the Aryan numerals before Greek was Greek, for thus only can we account for the coincidences as exhibited in the subjoined table.

If we cannot account for the coincidences between the French, Italian, Spanish, Portuguese, and Wallachian numerals, without admitting that all were derived from a common type, the Latin, the same conclusion is forced upon us by a comparison of the ancient numerals. They must have existed ready made in that language from which Sanskrit as well as Welsh is derived ; but only as far as hundred. Thousand had not received expression at that early period, and hence the names for thousand differ, not however without giving, by their very disagreement, some further indications as

	Sanskrit.	Greek.	Latin.	Lithuanian.	Gothic.
I.	ekas	εἷς (οὔη)	unus	wienas	ains
II.	dvau	δύω	duo	du	tvai
III.	trayas	τρεῖς	tres	trys	threis
IV.	katvâras	τέτταρες (Aeol., πισυρες)	quatuor (Oscan, petora)	keturi	fidvôr
V.	panka	πέντε	quinque (Oscan, pomtis)	penki	fimf
VI.	shash	ἕξ	sex	szeszi	saihs
VII.	sapta	ἑπτά	septem	septyni	sibun
VIII.	ashtau	ὀκτώ	octo	asztuni	ahtau
IX.	nava	ἐννέα	novem	dewyni	niun
X.	dasa	δέκα	decem	deszimt	taihun
XI.	ekâdasa	ἕνδεκα	undecim	wieno-lika	ain-lif
XII.	dvâdasa	δώδεκα	duodecim	dwy-lika	tva-lif
XX.	vinsati	εἴκοσι	viginti	dwi-deszimti	tvaitigjus
C.	satam	ἑκατόν	centum	szimtas	taihun taihund
M.	sahasram	χίλιοι	mille	tukstantis	thusundi.

to the subsequent history of the Aryan race. We see Sanskrit and Zend share the name for thousand in common (Sk. sahasra, Zend hazanra), which shows, that after the southern branch had been severed from the northern, the ancestors of the Brahmans and Zoroastrians continued united for a time by the ties of a common language. The same conclusion may be drawn from the agreement between the Gothic thusundi and the Old Prussian tûsimtons (acc.), the Lithuanian tukstantis, the Old Slavonic tüisasta; while the Greeks and the Romans stand apart from all the rest, and seem to have formed, each independently, their own name for thousand.

·This earliest period, then, previous to any national separation, is what I call the *mythopœic* period, for every one of these common Aryan words is, in a certain sense, a myth. These words were all originally appellative; they expressed one out of many attributes, which seemed characteristic of a certain object, and the selection of these attributes and their expression in language, represents a kind of unconscious poetry, which modern languages have lost altogether.

Language has been called fossil poetry. But as the artist does not know that the clay which he is handling contains the remnants of organic life, we do not feel that when we address a father, we call him protector, nor did the Greeks, when using the word δαήρ, brother-in-law, know that this term applied originally only to the younger brothers of the husband, who stayed at home with the bride while their elder brother was out in the field or the forests. The Sanskrit devar meant originally play-

mate [1]—it told its own story—it was a myth;
but in Greek it has dwindled down into a
mere name, or a technical term. Yet, even
in Greek it is not allowed to form a feminine
of δαήρ, as little as we should venture even
now to form a masculine of ' daughter.'

Soon, however, languages lose their etymological conscience, and thus we find in Latin
not only vidua, husbandless (Penelope tam
diu vidua viro suo caruit), but viduus, a
formation which, if analysed etymologically,
is as absurd as the Teutonic a widower.
But it must be confessed, that the Old Latin
viduus,[2] a name of Orcus, who had a temple
outside Rome, makes it doubtful whether
the Latin vidua is really the Sanskrit vidhavâ, however great their similarity ; unless
we admit that a verb viduare was derived
from vidua, and that afterwards a new
adjective was formed with a more general
sense, so that viduus to a Roman ear meant
nothing more than privatus.

But, it may be asked—how does the fact,
that the Aryan languages possess this
treasure of ancient names in common, or
even the discovery that all these names had
originally an expressive and poetical power,

[1] [Identical with the Greek δαϜήρ, from the root *div*,
to play (Curtius, i. 275), is the Latin *lēvir*. The letters
d and *l* often interchange, *e.g.* Lith.—*lika* (ten), Greek
δεκα ; *lacru-ma* and δάκρυ ; *dingua* and *lingua ;* Ulysses
and 'Οδυσσεύς ; *odor* and *olfacio, præsidium* and *præ-
silium.*]

[2] Hartung, *Die Religion der Römer*, ii. 90.

explain the phenomenon of mythological language among all the members of this family ? How does it render intelligible that phase of the human mind which gave birth to the extraordinary stories of gods and heroes—of gorgons and chimæras—of things that no human eye had ever seen, and that no human mind in a healthy state could ever have conceived ?

Before we can answer this question, we must enter into some more preliminary observations as to the formation of words. Tedious as this may seem, we believe that while engaged in these considerations, the mist of mythology will gradually clear away, and enable us to discover behind the floating clouds of the dawn of thought and language, that real nature which mythology has so long veiled and disguised.

All the common Aryan words which we have hitherto examined referred to definite objects. They are all substantives, in so far as expressing something substantial, something open to sensuous perception. Nor is it in the power of language to express originally anything except objects as nouns, and qualities as verbs. Hence, the only definition we can give of language during that early state is, that it is the conscious expression in sound, of impressions received by all the senses.

To us, abstract nouns are so familiar that we can hardly appreciate the difficulty which men experienced in forming them. We can scarcely imagine a language without abstract nouns. There are, however, dialects spoken at the present day which have no abstract nouns, and the more we go back in the history of languages, the smaller we find the number of these useful expressions. As far as language is concerned, an abstract word is nothing but an adjective raised into a substantive ; but in thought the conception of a quality as a subject, is a matter of extreme difficulty, and, in strict logical parlance, impossible. If we say, ' I love virtue,' we seldom connect any definite notion with virtue. Virtue is not a being, however unsubstantial ; it is nothing individual, personal, active ; nothing that could by itself produce an expressible impression on our mind. The word virtue is only a short-hand expression, and when men said for the first time ' I love virtue,' what they meant by it originally was ' I love all things that are virtuous.'

But there are other words, which we hardly call abstract, but which nevertheless were so originally, and are so still, in form ; I mean words like day and night, spring and winter, dawn and twilight, storm and thunder. For what do we mean if we speak of day and night, or of spring and winter ? We may answer, a season, or any other portion of time. But what is time, in our conceptions ? It is nothing substantial, nothing individual ; it is a quality raised by language into a substance. Therefore if we say ' the day dawns,' ' the night approaches,' we predicate actions of things that cannot act, we affirm a proposition which, if analysed logically, would have no definable subject.

The same applies to collective words, such as sky and earth, dew and rain—even to rivers and mountains. For if we say, ' the earth nourishes man,' we do not mean any tangible portion of soil, but the earth, conceived as a whole ; nor do we mean by the sky the small horizon which our eye can scan. We imagine something which does not fall under our senses, but whether we call it a whole, a power, or an idea, in speaking of it we change it unawares into something individual.

Now in ancient languages every one of these words had necessarily a termination expressive of gender, and this naturally produced in the mind the corresponding idea of sex, so that these names received not only an individual, but a sexual character. There was no substantive which was not either masculine or feminine ; neuters being of later growth, and distinguishable chiefly in the nominative.

What must have been the result of this ? As long as people thought in language, it was simply impossible to speak of morning or evening, of spring and winter, without giving to these conceptions something of an individual, active, sexual, and at last, personal character. They were either nothings, as they are nothings to our withered thought, or they were something ; and then they could not be conceived as mere powers, but as beings powerful. Even in our time, though we have the conception of nature as a power, what do we mean by power, except something powerful ? Now, in early language, nature was *Natura*, a mere adjective made substantive ; she was the Mother always ' going to bring forth.' Was this not a more definite idea than that which we connect with nature ? And let us look to our poets, who still think and feel in language—that is, who use no word without having really enlivened it in their mind, who do not trifle with language, and may in this sense be called μυθολογοι. Can they speak of nature and similar things as neutral powers, without doing violence to their feelings ? Let us open Wordsworth, and we shall hardly find him use an abstract term without some life and blood in it.

Religion.

Sacred Religion, mother of form and fear,
Dread arbitress of mutable respect,
New rites ordaining when the old are wrecked,
Or cease to please the fickle worshipper.

Winter.

Humanity, delighting to behold
A fond reflection of her own decay,

Hath painted Winter like a traveller old,
Propped on a staff, and, through the sullen day,
In hooded mantle, limping o'er the plain,
As though his weakness were disturbed by pain :
Or, if a juster fancy should allow
An undisputed symbol of command,
The chosen sceptre is a withered bough,
Infirmly grasped within a palsied hand.
These emblems suit the helpless and forlorn ;
But mighty Winter the device shall scorn.
For he it was—dread Winter !—who beset,
Flinging round van and rear his ghastly net,
That host, when from the regions of the Pole
They shrunk, insane Ambition's barren goal—
That host, as huge and strong as e'er defied
Their God, and placed their trust in human
     pride !
As fathers prosecute rebellious sons,
He smote the blossoms of their warrior youth ;
He called on *Frost's* inexorable tooth [1]
Life to consume in manhood's firmest hold . . . .
. . . And bade the *Snow* their ample backs
     bestride,
     And to the battle ride.

So, again, of *Age and Hours.*

Age ! twine thy brows with fresh spring flowers,
And call a train of laughing *Hours,*
And bid them dance, and bid them sing ;
And thou, too, mingle in the ring !

Now, when writing these lines, Wordsworth could hardly have thought of the
classical Horace : the conception of dancing
Hours came as natural to his mind as to
the poets of old.

[1] [Cf. *frigora mordent.*—Horace, *Satires,* ii. 6, 45,
and ' frost-bite.']

Or, again, of *Storms and Seasons.*

Ye *Storms*, resound the praises of your King !
And ye mild Seasons—in a sunny clime,
Midway, on some high hill, while father *Time*
Looks on delighted—meet in festal ring,
And loud and long of Winter's triumph sing!

We are wont to call this poetical diction,
and to make allowance for what seems to
us exaggerated language. But to the poet
it is no exaggeration, nor was it to the
ancient poets of language. Poetry is older
than prose, and abstract speech more difficult than the fulness of a poet's sympathy
with nature. It requires reflection to divest
nature of her living expression, to see in
the swift-riding clouds nothing but vapor-
ous exhalations, in the frowning mountains
masses of stone, and in the lightning electric
sparks. Wordsworth feels what he says
when he exclaims—

Mountains, and Vales, and Floods, I call on you
To share the passion of a just disdain ;

and when he speaks of ' the last hill that
parleys with the setting sun,' this expression
came to him as he was communing with
nature ; it was a thought untranslated as
yet into the prose of our traditional and
emaciated speech ; it was a thought such as
the men of old would not have been ashamed
of in their common conversation.

There are some poems of this modern
ancient, which are all mythology, and as we

shall have to refer to them hereafter, I shall give one more extract, which to a Hindu and an ancient Greek would have been more intelligible than it is to us.

Hail, orient Conqueror of gloomy Night !
Thou that canst shed the bliss of gratitude
On hearts, howe'er insensible or rude ;
Whether thy punctual visitations smite
The haughty towers where monarchs dwell,
Or thou, impartial Sun, with presence bright
Cheer'st the low threshold of the peasant's cell !
Not unrejoiced I see thee climb the sky,
In naked splendour, clear from mist and haze,
Or cloud approaching to divert the rays,
Which even in deepest winter testify
   Thy power and majesty,
Dazzling the vision that presumes to gaze.
Well does thine aspect usher in this Day ;
As aptly suits therewith that modest pace
   Submitted to the chains
That bind thee to the path which God ordains !
   That thou shouldst trace,
Till, with the heavens and earth, thou pass
   away !
Nor less, the stillness of these frosty plains—
Their utter stillness, and the silent grace
Of yon ethereal summits, white with snow,
(Whose tranquil pomp and spotless purity
   Report of storms gone by
   To us who tread below)—
Do with the service of this Day accord.
Divinest object which th' uplifted eye
Of mortal man is suffered to behold ;
Thou, who upon these snow-clad Heights hast
   poured
Meek lustre, nor forget'st the humble Vale ;
Thou who dost warm Earth's universal mould,

And for thy bounty wert not unadored
  By pious men of old ;
Once more, heart-cheering Sun, I bid thee hail !
Bright be thy course to-day—let not this
    promise fail ! [1]

Why then, if we ourselves, in speaking of
the Sun or the Storms, of Sleep and Death,
of Earth and Dawn, connect either no
distinct idea at all with these names, or
allow them to cast over our mind the fleeting shadows of the poetry of old ; why, if
we, when speaking with the warmth which
is natural to the human heart, call upon
the Winds and the Sun, the Ocean and the
Sky, as if they would still hear us ; why, if
plastic thought cannot represent any one of
these beings or powers, without giving them,
if not a human form, at least human life
and human feeling—why should we wonder
at the ancients, with their language throb-
bing with life and revelling in colour, if
instead of the grey outlines of our modern
thought, they threw out those living forms
of nature, endowed with human powers,
nay, with powers more than human, inasmuch as the light of the Sun was brighter
than the light of a human eye, and the
roaring of the Storms louder than the shouts
of the human voice. We may be able to
account for the origin of rain and dew, of
storm and thunder ; yet, to the great
majority of mankind, all these things, unless

[1] [*Thanksgiving Ode*, January 18, 1816, *sub. init.*]

they are mere names, are still what they were to Homer, only perhaps less beautiful, less poetical, less real, and living.

So much for that peculiar difficulty which the human mind experiences in speaking of collective or abstract ideas—a difficulty which, as we shall see, will explain many of the difficulties of Mythology.

We have now to consider a similar feature of ancient languages—the auxiliary verbs. They hold the same position among verbs, as abstract nouns among substantives. They are of later origin, and had all originally a more material and expressive character. Our auxiliary verbs have had to pass through a long chain of vicissitudes before they arrived at the withered and lifeless form which fits them so well for the purposes of our abstract prose. Habere, which is now used in all the Romance languages simply to express a past tense, *j'ai aimé,* I loved, was originally, to hold fast, to hold back, as we may see in its derivative, habenæ, the reins. Thus tenere, to hold, becomes, in Spanish, an auxiliary verb, that can be used very much in the same manner as habere. The Greek ἔχω is the Sanskrit sah, and meant originally, to be strong, to be able, or to can. The Latin fui, I was, the Sanskrit bhû, to be, corresponds to the Greek φύω, and there shows still its original and material power of growing, in an intransitive and transitive sense.

As, the radical of the Sanskrit as-mi, the Greek ἐμ-μί, the Lithuanian as-mi, I am, is probably connected with another root, âs, to sit, which we see in Greek ἧσ-ται, Sanskrit âs-te. Stare, to stand, sinks down in the Romance dialects to a mere auxiliary, as in *j'ai été*, I have been, *i.e.* habeo statum, I have stood ; j'ai-été convaincu, I have stood convinced ; the phonetic change of statum into été being borne out by the transition of status into état. The German werden, which is used to form futures and passives, the Gothic varth, points back to the Sanskrit vrit, the Latin verto. Will, again, in *he will go*, has lost its radical meaning of wishing ; and shall, used in the same tense, *I shall go*, hardly betrays, even to the etymologist, its original power of legal or moral obligation. *Schuld*, however, in German means debt and sin, and *soll* has there not yet taken a merely temporal signification, the first trace of which may be discovered, however, in the names of the three Teutonic Parcæ. These are called *Vurdh, Vurdhandi,* and *Skuld*—Past, Present, and Future.[1] But what could be the original conception of a verb which, even in its earliest application, has already the abstract meaning of moral duty or legal obligation ? Where could language, which can only draw upon the material world for

[1] Kuhn, *Zeitschrift für vergleichende Sprachforschung*, iii. 449.

its nominal and verbal treasures, find something analogous to the abstract idea of He shall pay, or, He ought to yield ? Grimm, who has endeavoured to follow the German language into its most secret recesses, proposes an explanation of this verb, which deserves serious consideration, however strange and incredible it may appear at first sight.

Shall, and its preterite *should*, have the following forms in Gothic :—

Present.	Preterite.
Skal	Skulda
Skalt	Skuldês
Skal	Skulda
Skulum	Skuldedum
Skuluþ	Skuldeduþ
Skulun	Skuldedun

In Gothic this verb skal, which seems to be a present, can be proved to be an old perfect, analogous to Greek perfects like οἶδα, which have the form of a perfect but the power of the present. There are several verbs of the same character in the German language, and in English they can be detected by the absence of the *s*, as the termination of the third person singular of the present. Skal, then, according to Grimm, means, 'I owe, I am bound,' but originally it meant, 'I have killed.' The chief guilt punished by ancient Teutonic law, was the guilt of manslaughter—and in many cases it could be atoned for by a fine.

Hence, skal meant literally, 'I am guilty'
(ich bin schuldig); and afterwards, when this
full expression had been ground down into
a legal phrase, new expressions became possible, such as, 'I have killed a free man, a
serf,' *i.e.* 'I am guilty of a free man, a serf,'
and at last, 'I owe (the fine for having
slain) a free man, a serf.' In this manner
Grimm accounts for the still later and more
anomalous expressions, such as 'he shall
pay,' *i.e.* 'he is guilty to pay' (er ist schuldig
zu zahlen); 'he shall go,' *i.e.* 'he must go,'
and last, 'I shall withdraw,' *i.e.* 'I feel bound
to withdraw.' [1]

A change of meaning like this seems, no
doubt, violent and fanciful, but we should
feel more inclined to accept it, if we considered how almost every word we use discloses similar changes as soon as we analyse
it etymologically, and then follow gradually
its historical growth. If we say, 'I am
obliged to go,' or, 'I am bound to pay, 'we
forget that the origin of these expressions
carries us back to times when men were

---

[1] [The root *skal* probably meant at first to stumble
or trip, akin to *sphal*, to stumble and *fall*, then to make
a *faux pas*, offend or fail, then to be guilty or bound
to pay. *Cf.* Lat. *scel-us*, Ger. *schul-d*, debt, crime
(Curtius, i. 453), so 'guilty' (Anglo-Sax. *gylt-ig*) means
bound to pay (Anglo-Sax. *gyld-an*, to pay). *Cf.* 'guilty of
death'—S. Matt. xxvi. 66 (ἔνοχος θανάτου), *i.e.* bound
to pay (the penalty of) death, and debtors (ὀφειλέται)—
S. Luke xiii. 4, for sinners; *ought* said of action which
is *owing* or one is *obliged* (*obligatus*), tied, or *bound* to
do; Greek δεῖ, it binds me, I ought.]

F

bound to go, or bound over to pay. 'Hoc me fallit' means, in Latin, 'it deceives me,' 'it escapes me.' Afterwards, it took the sense of 'it is removed from me,' 'I want it,' 'I must have it': and hence, *il me faut*, I must. Again, *I may* is the Gothic.

Mag, maht, mag, magum, maguþ, magun,

and its primary signification was, 'I am strong.' Now, this verb also was originally a preterite, and derived from a root which meant, to beget, whence the Gothic *magus*, son (*i.e.* begotten), the Scotch *Mac*, and Gothic *magaths*, daughter, the English *maid*.

In mythological language we must make due allowance for the absence of merely auxiliary words. Every word, whether noun or verb, had still its full original power during the mythopœic ages. Words were heavy and unwieldy. They said more than they ought to say, and hence, much of the strangeness of the mythological language, which we can only understand by watching the natural growth of speech. Where we speak of the sun following the dawn, the ancient poets could only speak and think of the sun loving and embracing the dawn. What is with us a sunset, was to them the Sun growing old, decaying, or dying. Our sunrise was to them the Night giving birth to a brilliant child ; and in the Spring they really saw the Sun or the Sky embracing the earth with a warm embrace, and showering treasures into the lap of nature. There are many myths in Hesiod, of late origin, where we have only to replace a full verb by an auxiliary, in order to change mythical into logical language. Hesiod calls Nyx (Night) the mother of Moros (Fate), and the dark Kêr (Destruction) ; of Thanatos (Death), Hypnos (Sleep), and the tribe of the Oneiroi (Dreams). And this her progeny she is said to have borne without a father. Again, she is called the mother of Mômos (Blame), and of the woeful Oizys (Woe), and of the Hesperides (Evening Stars), who guard the beautiful golden apples on the other side of the far-famed Okeanos, and the trees that bear fruit. She also bore Nemesis (Vengeance), and Apatê (Fraud), and Philotês (Lust), and the pernicious Geras (Old Age), and the strong-minded Eris (Strife). Now, let us use our modern expressions, such as ' the stars are seen as the night approaches,' ' we sleep,' ' we dream,' ' we die,' ' we run danger during night,' ' nightly revels lead to strife, angry discussions, and woe,' ' many nights bring old age, and at last death,' ' an evil deed concealed at first by the darkness of night will at last be revealed by the day,' ' Night herself will be revenged on the criminal,' and we have translated the language of Hesiod—a language to a great extent understood by the people whom he addressed—into our modern form of thought and speech.[1] All this is hardly mythological language, but rather a poetical and proverbial kind of expression known to all poets, whether modern or ancient, and frequently to be found in the language of common people.

Uranos, in the language of Hesiod, is used as a name for the sky ; he is made or born that ' he should be a firm place for the blessed gods.'[2] It is said twice, that Uranos covers everything (v. 127), and that when he brings the night he is stretched out everywhere, embracing the earth. This sounds almost as if the Greek myth had still preserved a recollection of the etymological power of Uranos. For Uranos is the Sanskrit Varu*n*a, and this is derived from a root VAR, to cover ; Varu*n*a being in the *Veda* also a name of the firmament, but especially connected with the night, and opposed to Mitra, the day.[3] At all

---

[1] As to Philotes being the Child of Night, Juliet understood what it meant when she said—
  ' Spread thy close curtain, love-performing Night !
  That unawares, eyes may wink ; and Romeo
  Leap to these arms, untalked of and unseen !—
  Lovers can see to do their amorous rites
  By their own beauties ; or, if Love be blind,
  It best agrees with Night.'

[2] Hesiod, *Theog.* 128—
  Γαῖα δέ τοι πρῶτον μὲν ἐγείνατο ἶσον ἑαυτῇ
  Οὐρανὸν ἀστερόενθ', ἵνα μιν περὶ πάντα καλύπτοι,
  ὄφρ' εἴη μακάρεσσι θεοῖς ἕδος ἀσφαλὲς αἰεί.

[3] [Very similarly *kamui*, the Ainu's word for god, meant primarily ' that which covers,' heaven, as the great overshadowing lord of all—J. Batchelor, *The Ainu and their Folk-lore*, 580.]

events, the name of Uranos recalled to the Greek something of its usual meaning, and when we see him called ἀστερόεις, the starry heaven, which was not the case with names like Apollo or Dionysos, we can hardly believe, as Mr. Grote says, that to the Greek, ' Uranos, Nyx, Hypnos, and Oneiros (Heaven, Night, Sleep, and Dream) are persons, just as much as Zeus and Apollo.' We need only read a few lines further in Hesiod, in order to see that the progeny of Gæa, of which Uranos is the first, has not yet altogether arrived at that mythological personification or crystallisation which makes most of the Olympian gods so difficult and doubtful in their original character. The poet has asked the Muses in the introduction how the gods and the earth were first born, and the rivers and the endless sea, and the bright stars, and the wide heaven above ' (οὐρανὸς εὐρὺς ὕπερθεν). The whole poem of the *Theogony* is an answer to this question ; and we can hardly doubt therefore that the Greek saw in some of the names that follow, simply poetical conceptions of real objects, such as the earth, and the rivers, and the mountains. Uranos, the first offspring of Gæa, is afterwards raised into a deity—endowed with human feelings and attributes ; but, the very next offspring of Gæa, Οὐρέα μακρά, the great Mountains, are even in language represented as neuter, and can therefore hardly claim to be considered as persons like Zeus and Apollo.

Mr. Grote goes too far in insisting on the purely literal meaning of the whole of Greek mythology. Some mythological figures of speech remained in the Greek language to a very late period, and were perfectly understood—that is to say, they required as little explanation as our expressions of ' the sun sets,' or ' the sun rises.' Mr. Grote feels compelled to admit this, but he declines to draw any further conclusions from it. ' Although some of the attributes and actions ascribed to these persons,' he says, ' are often explicable by allegory, the whole series and system of them never are so : the theorist who adopts this course of explanation finds that, after one or two simple and obvious steps, the path is no longer open, and he is forced to clear a way for himself by gratuitous refinements and conjectures.' Here, then, Mr. Grote admits what he calls allegory as an ingredient of mythology ; still he makes no further use of it, and leaves the whole of mythology as a riddle, that cannot and ought not to be solved, as something irrational—as a past that was never present, declining even to attempt a partial explanation of this important problem in the history of the Greek mind. Such a want of scientific courage would have put a stop to many systems which have since grown to completeness, but which at first had to make the most timid and uncertain steps. In palæontological sciences we must learn to ignore certain things ; and what Suetonius says of the grammarian, ' boni grammatici est nonnulla etiam nescire,' applies with particular force to the mythologist. It is in vain to attempt to solve the secret of every name ; and nobody has expressed this with greater modesty than he who has laid the most lasting foundation of Comparative Mythology. Grimm, in the introduction to his *German Mythology*, says, without disguise, ' I shall indeed interpret all that I can, but I cannot interpret all that I should like.' But surely Otfried Müller had opened a path into the labyrinth of Greek mythology, which a scholar of Mr. Grote's power and genius might have followed, and which at least he ought to have proved as either right or wrong. How late mythological language was in vogue among the Greeks has been shown by O. Müller (p. 65) in the myth of Kyrene. The Greek town of Kyrene in Libya was founded about Olymp. 37 ; the ruling race derived its origin from the Minyans, who reigned chiefly in Iolkos, in Southern Thessaly ; the foundation of the colony was due to the oracle of Apollo at Pytho. Hence, the myth—' The heroic maid Kyrene, who lived in Thessaly, is loved by Apollo and carried off to Libya ; ' while in modern language we should say—' The town of Kyrene, in Thessaly, sent a colony to Libya, under the auspices of Apollo.' Many more instances might be given, where the mere substitution of a more matter-of-fact verb divests a myth at once of its miraculous appearance.[1]

Kaunos is called the son of Miletos, *i.e.* Kretan colonists from Miletos had founded the town of Kaunos in Lycia. Again, the myth says that Kaunos fled from Miletos to Lycia, and his sister Byblos was changed, by sorrow over her lost brother, into a fountain. Here Miletos in Ionia, being better known than the Miletos in Kreta, has been brought in by mistake, Byblos being simply a small river near the Ionian Miletos. Again, Pausanias tells us as a matter of history, that Miletos, a beautiful boy, fled from Kreta to Ionia, in order to escape the jealousy of Minos—the fact being, that Miletos in Ionia was a colony of Miletos of Kreta, and Minos the most famous King of Kreta. Again, Marpessa is called the daughter of Evenos—and a myth represents her as carried away by Idas—Idas being the name of a famous hero of the town of Marpessa. The fact, implied by the myth and confirmed by other evidence, is, that colonists started from the river Evenos, and founded Marpessa in Messina.

[1] Kanne's *Mythology*, § 10, p. xxxii.

And here again, the myth adds, that Evenos, after trying in vain to reconquer his daughter from Idas, was changed by sorrow into a river, like Byblos, the sister of Miletos.

If the Hellenes call themselves αὐτόχθονες, we fancy we understand what is meant by this .expression. But, if we are informed that πύρρα was the oldest name of Thessaly, and that Hellen was the son of Pyrrha, Mr. Grote would say that we have here to deal with a myth, and that the Greeks at least, never doubted that there really was one individual called Pyrrha, and another called Hellen. Now, this may be true with regard to the later Greeks, such as Homer and Hesiod ;—but was it so—could it have been so originally ? Language is always language—it always meant something originally, and he, whoever it was, who first, instead of calling the Hellenes born of the soil, spoke of Pyrrha, the mother of Hellen, must have meant something intelligible and rational, he could not have meant a friend of his whom he knew by the name of Hellen, and an old lady called Pyrrha ; he meant what we mean if we speak of Italy as the mother of Art.

Even in more modern times than those of which Otfried Müller speaks—we find that 'to speak mythologically,' was the fashion among poets and philosophers. Pausanias complains of those ' who genealogise everything, and make Pythis the son of Delphos.'

The story of Eros in the Phædros is called a myth (μῦθος, 254 D, λόγος, 257 B);—yet Sokrates says ironically—'that it is one of those which you may believe or not (τούτοις δὴ ἔξεστι μὲν πείθεσθαι, ἔξεστι δὲ μή). Again, when he tells the story of the Egyptian god Theuth, he calls it a 'tradition of old' (ἀκοήν γ' ἔχω λέγειν τῶν προτέρων), but Phædros knows at once that it is one of Sokrates' own making, and he says to him, 'Sokrates, thou makest easily Egyptian or any other stories' (λόγοι). When Pindar calls Apophasis the daughter of Epimetheus, every Greek understood this mythological language as well as if he had said 'an after-thought leads to an excuse.' [1] Nay, even in Homer, when the lame Litae (Prayers) are said to follow Atê (Fate), trying to appease her, a Greek understood this language as well as we do, when we say that 'Hell is paved with good intentions.'

When Prayers are called the daughters of Zeus, we are hardly as yet within the sphere

[1] O. Müller has pointed out how the different parents given to the *Erinyes* by different poets were suggested by the character which each poet ascribed to them. 'Evidently,' he says, in his *Essay on the Eumenides*, p. 184, 'this genealogy answered better to the views and poetical objects of Æschylos than one of the current genealogies by which the Erinyes are derived from Skotos and Gæa (Sophokles), Kronos and Eurynome (in a work ascribed to Epimenides), Phorkys (Euphorion), Gæa Eurynome (Istron), Acheron and Night (Eudemos), Hades and Persephone (Orphic hymns), Hades and Styx (Athenodoros and Mnaseas). See, however, *Ares*, by H. D. Müller, p. 67.

of pure mythology. For Zeus was to the Greeks the protector of the supplices, Ζεὺς ἱκετέσιος—and hence prayers are called his daughters, as we might call Liberty the daughter of England, or Prayer the off-spring of the soul.

All these sayings, however, though mythical, are not yet myths. It is the essential character of a true myth that it should no longer be intelligible by a reference to the spoken language. The plastic character of ancient language, which we have traced in the formation of nouns and verbs, is not sufficient to explain how a myth could have lost its expressive power or its consciousness. Making due allowance for the difficulty of forming abstract nouns and abstract verbs, we should yet be unable to account for anything beyond allegorical poetry among the nations of antiquity ; mythology would still remain a riddle. Here, then, we must call to our aid another powerful ingredient in the formation of ancient speech, for which I find no better name than *Polyonymy* and *Synonymy*.[1] Most nouns, as we have seen before, were originally appellatives or predicates, expressive of what seemed at the time the most characteristic attribute of an object. But as most objects have more than one attribute, and as, under different aspects, one or the other attribute might

[1] See the author's letter to Chev. Bunsen, *On the Turanian Languages*, p. 35.

seem more appropriate to form the name, it happened by necessity that most objects, during the early period of language, had more than one name. In the course of time, the greater portion of these names became useless, and they were mostly replaced in literary dialects by one fixed name, which might be called the proper name of such objects. The more ancient a language, the richer it is in synonyms.

Synonyms, again, if used constantly, must naturally give rise to a number of homonyms. If we may call the sun by fifty names expressive of different qualities, some of these names will be applicable to other objects also which happen to possess the same quality. These different objects would then be called by the same name—they would become homonyms.

In the *Veda*, the earth is called urvî (wide), p*r*ithvî (broad), mahî (great), and many more names of which the Nigha*nt*u mentions twenty-one. These twenty-one words would be synonyms. But urvî (wide) is not only given as a name of the earth, but also means a river. P*r*ithvî (broad) means not only earth, but sky and dawn. Mahî (great, strong) is used for cow and speech, as well for earth. Hence, earth, river, sky, dawn, cow, and speech, would become homonyms. All these names, however, are simple and intelligible. But most of the old terms, thrown out by language at the first burst of youthful poetry, are based on bold metaphors. These metaphors once forgotten, or the meaning of the roots whence the words were derived once dimmed and changed, many of these words would naturally lose their radical as well as their poetical meaning. They would become mere names handed down in the conversation of a family ; understood, perhaps, by the grandfather, familiar to the father, but strange to the son, and misunderstood by the grandson. This misunderstanding may arise in various manners. Either the radical meaning of a word is forgotten, and thus what was originally an appellative, or a name, in the etymological sense of the word (nomen stands for gnomen, quo gnoscimus res, like natus for gnatus), dwindled down into a mere sound—a name in the modern sense of the word. Thus ζεύς, being originally a name of the sky, like the Sanskrit dyáus, became gradually a proper name, which betrayed its appellative meaning only in a few proverbial expressions, such as ζεύς ύει, or 'sub Jove frigido.'

Frequently it happened that after the true etymological meaning of a word had been forgotten, a new meaning was attached to it by a kind of etymological instinct which exists even in modern languages. Thus, Λυκηγενής, the son of light—Apollo, was changed into a son of Lycia ; Δήλιος, the bright one, gave rise to the myth of the birth of Apollo in Delos.

Again, where two names existed for the same object, two persons would spring up out of the two names, and as the same stories could be told of either, they would naturally be represented as brothers and sisters—as parent and child. Thus we find Selene, the moon, side by side with Mene, the moon ; Helios, the Sun, and Phœbos ; and in most of the Greek heroes we can discover humanised forms of Greek gods, with names which, in many instances, were epithets of their divine prototypes. Still more frequently it happened that adjectives connected with a word as applied to one object, were used with the same word even though applied to a different object. What was told of the Sea was told of the Sky, and the Sun once being called a lion or a wolf, was soon endowed with claws and mane, even where the animal metaphor was forgotten. Thus the Sun with his golden rays might be called ' golden-handed,' *hand* being expressed by the same word as *ray*.[1] But when the same epithet was applied to

[1] [See also M. Müller, *Science of Language*, eighth ed., ii. 414–415. The same conception was formed by the ancient Egyptians. The sun is depicted in the tomb of Aï, Tell el Amarna, pouring down his rays upon King Khûenaten and his family, each ray terminating in a hand, which is shedding abroad life (*ankh*) and blessing ; see Wiedemann, *Religion of the Ancient Egyptians*, p. 37, fig. 11 ; and Erman, *Handbook of*

Apollo or Indra, a myth would spring up, as we find it in German and Sanskrit mythology, telling us that Indra lost his hand, and that it was replaced by a hand made of gold.

Here we have some of the keys to mythology, but the manner of handling them can only be learnt from comparative philology. As in French it is difficult to find the radical meaning of many a word, unless we compare it with its corresponding forms in Italian, Spanish, or Provençal ; we should find it impossible to discover the origin of many a Greek word, without comparing it with its more or less corrupt relatives in German, Latin, Slavonic, and Sanskrit. Unfortunately we have in this ancient circle of languages nothing corresponding to Latin, by which we can test the more or less original form of a word in French, Italian, and Spanish. Sanskrit is not the mother of Latin and Greek, as Latin is the mother of French and Italian. But although Sanskrit is but one among many sisters—it is no doubt the eldest—in so far as it has preserved its words in their most primitive

Egyptian Religion, p. 69, fig. 48. Similarly Longfellow says that the moon—

' Titan-like stretches its hundred hands upon mountain and meadow.'—*Evangeline*, I. v.

' Long-handed ' or ' long-armed ' was a title given to Lugh, the Irish sun hero (J. Rhys, *Celtic Heathendom*, 397.]

state ; and if we once succeed in tracing a Latin and Greek word to its corresponding form in Sanskrit, we are generally able at the same time to account for its formation, and to fix its radical meaning. What should we know of the original meaning of πατήρ, μήτηρ, and θυγάτηρ,[1] if we were reduced to the knowledge of one language like Greek ? But as soon as we trace these words to Sanskrit, their primitive power is clearly indicated. O. Müller was one of the first to see and acknowledge that classical philology must surrender all etymological research to comparative philology, and that the origin of Greek words cannot be settled by a mere reference to Greek. This applies with particular force to mythological names. In order to become mythological, it was necessary that the radical meaning of certain names should have been obscured and forgotten in the language to which they belong. Thus what is mythological in one language, is frequently natural and intelligible in another. We say, ' the sun sets,' but in our own Teutonic mythology, a seat or throne is given to the sun on which he sits down, as in Greek Eos is called χρυσόθρονος, or as the Modern Greek speaks

---

[1] Here is a specimen of Greek etymology, from the *Etymologicum Magnum :* Θυγάτηρ, παρὰ τὸ θύειν καὶ ὁρμᾶν κατὰ γαστρὸς· ἐκ τοῦ θύω καὶ τοῦ γαστήρ· λέγεται γὰρ τὰ θήλεα τάχιον κινεῖσθαι ἐν τῇ μήτρᾳ.

of the setting sun as ἥλιος βασιλεύει.[1] We
doubt about Hekate, but we understand
at once Ἕκατος and Ἑκατηβόλος. We hesitate
about Lucina, but we accept immediately

[1] [This beautiful and highly poetical conception of
the sunset, to express the kingly pomp and splendour
of the sinking luminary, ' He is in his majesty' (see
M. Constantinides, *Neohellenica*, 393), is common to
many languages. Ramses III. says, ' I was crowned
with the robes of State, like Tum,' the setting sun
(*Harris Papyrus*). *Cf.* the following :—

> ' The sun unwilling leaves
> So dear a picture of his sovereign power,
> And I could witness his most kingly hour.'
> —Keats, *Endymion.*

> ' I watch'd the great red sun, in clouds, go down,
> An orient king, that 'mid his bronzèd slaves
> Dies, leaning on his sceptre, with his crown.'
> —W. M. W. Call, *Golden Histories* (1871).

' At thy extinction thou clothest thyself in thy most
gorgeous of raiments.'—Arabic poet 'Uiwan (Goldziher,
Myth. of the Hebrews, 95).

' Glorious summer twilights when the sun, like a
proud Conqueror and Imperial Taskmaster, turned his
back, with his gold-purple emblazonry, and all his
fire-clad body-guard.'—Carlyle, *Sartor Resartus*, bk. ii.
ch. 2.

With *o iglio vasileggui*, ' the sun is kingly,' the
Calabrian's periphrase for sunset, the Countess Cesaresco
compares the simile of a German poet :—

> ' Wie herrlich die Sonne dort untergeht,
> So stirbt ein Held ! '

> [How lordly doth yon sun go down
> As when a hero dies.]
> — *Study of Folk-Songs*, 170.

Thomson says that the shifting clouds at sunset

> ' In all their pomp attend his setting throne.'
> —*Summer.*

The Assyrians called the western abode of Shamash

what is a mere contraction of Lucna, the Latin Luna.   What is commonly called Hindu mythology, is of little or no avail for comparative purposes.   The stories of Siva, Vish*n*u, Mahâdeva, Pârvati, Kali, K*r*ish*n*a, &c., are of late growth, indigenous to India, and full of wild and fanciful conceptions.   But while this late mythology of the Purâ*n*as and even of the Epic poems, offers no assistance to the comparative mythologist, a whole world of primitive, natural, and intelligible mythology has been preserved to us in the *Veda*.   The mythology of the *Veda* is to comparative mythology what Sanskrit has been to comparative grammar.   There is, fortunately, no system of religion or mythology in the *Veda*.   Names are used in one hymn as appellatives, in another as names of gods.   The same god is sometimes represented as supreme, sometimes as equal, sometimes as inferior to others.   The whole nature of these so-called

(the sun) his Palace, *kummu.*—Sayce, *Hibbert Lectures*, 171.

The same gorgeous retinue which surrounds him when retiring to his pavilion of rest in the evening attends him when issuing from the eastern gate.

'Where the great sun begins his state.'

Gawin Douglas speaks of

'The cummyng of this kyng,
Newly aryssyn in hys estait ryall.'
—*Proloug of XII. Buk of Eneados*,
l. 277 (1513).

'Yonder comes the powerful king of day
Rejoicing in the East.'
—Thomson, *Seasons.*]

gods is still transparent; their first conception, in many cases, clearly perceptible. There are as yet no genealogies, no settled marriages between gods and goddesses. The father is sometimes the son, the brother is the husband, and she who in one hymn is the mother, is in another the wife. As the conceptions of the poet varied, so varied the nature of these gods. Nowhere is the wide distance which separates the ancient poems of India from the most ancient literature of Greece more clearly felt than when we compare the growing myths of the *Veda* with the full-grown and decayed myths on which the poetry of Homer is founded. The *Veda* is the real Theogony of the Aryan races, while that of Hesiod is a distorted caricature of the original image. If we want to know whither the human mind, though endowed with the natural consciousness of a divine power, is driven necessarily and inevitably by the irresistible force of language as applied to supernatural and abstract ideas, we must read the *Veda ;* and if we want to tell the Hindus what they are worshipping —mere names of natural phenomena, gradually obscured, personified, and deified—we must make them read the *Veda*. It was a mistake of the early Fathers to treat the Heathen gods [1] as demons or evil spirits,

[1] Aristotle has given an opinion of the Greek gods in a passage of the *Metaphysics*. He is attacking the Platonic ideas, and tries to show their contradictory character, calling them αἰσθητὰ ἀίδια, eternal un-

and we must take care not to commit the same error with regard to the Hindu god. Their gods have no more right to any substantive existence than Eos or Hemera—than Nyx or Apatê. They are masks without an actor—the creations of man, not his creators; they are nomina, not numina; names without being, not beings without names.

In some instances, no doubt, it happens that a Greek, or a Latin, or a Teutonic myth, may be explained, from the resources which each of these languages still possesses, as there are many words in Greek which can be explained etymologically without any reference to Sanskrit or Gothic. We shall begin with some of these myths, and then proceed to the more difficult, which must receive light from more distant regions, whether from the snowy rocks of Iceland and the songs of the *Edda*, or from the borders of the 'Seven Rivers,' and the hymns of the *Veda*.

The rich imagination, the quick perception, the intellectual vivacity, and ever-varying fancy of the Greek nation, make it easy to understand that, after the separation of the Aryan race, no language was richer, no mythology more varied, than that of the Greeks. Words were created with wonder-

eternals, *i.e.* things that cannot have any real existence; as men, he adds, maintain that there are gods, but give them a human form, thus making them really 'immortal mortals,' *i.e.* non-entities.

ful facility, and were forgotten again with that carelessness which the consciousness of inexhaustible power imparts to men of genius. The creation of every word was originally a poem, embodying a bold metaphor or a bright conception.[1] But, like the popular poetry of Greece, these words, if they were adopted by tradition, and lived on in the language of a family, of a city, of a tribe, in the dialects, or in the national speech of Greece, soon forgot the father that had given them birth, or the poet to whom they owed their existence. Their genealogical descent and native character were unknown to the Greeks themselves, and their etymological meaning would have baffled the most ingenious antiquarian. The Greeks, however, cared as little about the etymological individuality of their words as they cared to know the name of every bard that had first sung the Aristeia of Menelaos or Diomedes. One Homer was enough to satisfy their curiosity, and any etymology that explained any part of the meaning of a word was welcome, no historical con-

---

[1] [So Archbishop Trench : ‘ Language is fossil poetry ; in other words, we are not to look for the poetry which a people may possess only in its poems, or its poetical customs, traditions, and beliefs. Many a single word also is itself a concentrated poem, having stores of poetical thought and imagery laid up in it.’—*Study of Words*, p. 5 (ed. Routledge). And Carlyle : ‘ For every word we have there was a man and poet. The coldest word was once a glowing new metaphor, and bold questionable originality.’—*Past and Present*, ch. xvii.]

siderations being ever allowed to interfere with ingenious guesses. It is known how Sokrates changes, on the spur of the moment, Eros into a god of wings, but Homer is quite as ready with etymologies, and they are useful, at least so far as they prove that the real etymology of the names of the gods had been forgotten long before Homer.

We can best enter into the original meaning of a Greek myth, when some of the persons who act in it have preserved names intelligible in Greek. When we find the names of Eos, Selene, Helios, or Herse, we have words which tell their own story, and we have a ποῦ στῶ for the rest of the myth. Let us take the beautiful myth of Selene and Endymion. Endymion is the son of Zeus and Kalyke, but he is also the son of Aethlios, a king of Elis, who is himself called a son of Zeus, and whom Endymion is said to have succeeded as King of Elis. This localises our myth, and shows, at least, that Elis is its birthplace, and that, according to Greek custom, the reigning race of Elis derived its origin from Zeus. The same custom prevailed in India, and gave rise to the two great royal families of ancient India —the so-called Solar and the Lunar races: and Purûravas, of whom more by and by, says of himself—

> ' The great king of day
> And monarch of the night are my progenitors ;
> Their grandson I. . . .'

There may, then, have been a King of Elis, Aethlios, and he may have had a son, Endymion ; but what the myth tells of Endymion could not have happened to the King of Elis. The myth transfers Endymion into Karia, to Mount Latmos, because it was in the Latmian cave that Selene saw the beautiful sleeper, loved him and lost him. Now about the meaning of Selene, there can be no doubt ; but even if tradition had only preserved her other name, Asterodia, we should have had to translate this synonym, as Moon, as ' Wanderer among the stars.' But who is Endymion ? It is one of the many names of the sun, but with special reference to the setting or dying sun. It is derived from ἐν-δύω, a verb which, in classical Greek, is never used for setting, because the simple verb δύω had become the technical term for sunset. Δυσμαὶ ἡλίου, the setting of the sun, is opposed to ἀνατόλαι, the rising. Now, δύω meant, originally, to dive into ; and expressions like ἠέλιος δ' ἄρ ἔδυ, the sun dived, presupposes an earlier conception of ἔδυ πόντον, he dived into the sea. Thus Thetis addresses her companions, *Il.* xviii. 140—

Ὑμεῖς μὲν νῦν δῦτε θαλάσσης εὐρέα κόλπον.

(You may now dive into the broad bosom of the sea.)

Other dialects, particularly of maritime nations, have the same expression. In

Latin we find,[1] ' Cur *mergat* seras aequore flammas.' In Old Norse, ' Sôl gengr i aegi ' [The sun goes into the sea—Vigfusson, *Icel. Dict.*, p. 758.] Slavonic nations represent the sun as a woman stepping into her bath in the evening, and rising refreshed and purified in the morning ; or they speak of the Sea as the mother of the Sun, and of the Sun as sinking into her mother's arms at night.   We may suppose, therefore, that in some Greek dialect ἐνδύω was used in the same sense ; and that from ἐνδύω, ἐνδύμα was formed to express sunset.   From this was formed, ἐνδυμίων,[2] like οὐρανίων from οὐρανός, and like most of the names of the Greek months.   If ἐνδύμα had become a common name for sunset, the myth of Endymion could never have arisen.   But the original meaning of Endymion being once forgotten, what was told originally of the setting sun was now told of a name, which, in order to have any meaning, had to be changed into a god or a hero.   The setting sun *once* slept in the Latmian cave, the cave of night—Latmos being derived from the same root as Leto, Latona, the night ;—but *now* he sleeps on Mount Latmos, in Karia.   Endymion, sinking into eternal sleep after a life of but one day, was *once*

---

1 Grimm's *Mythology*, p. 704 [p. 742, ed. Stallybrass.]
2 Lauer, in his *System of Greek Mythology*, explains Endymion as the Diver. Gerhard in his *Greek Mythology* gives Ἐνδυμίων as ὁ ἐν δύμῃ ὤν.

the setting sun, the son of Zeus—the brilliant Sky, and Kalyke—the covering night (from καλύπτω) ; or, according to another saying, of Zeus and Protogeneia, the first-born goddess, or the Dawn, who is always represented, either as the mother, the sister, or the forsaken wife of the Sun. *Now* he is the son of a King of Elis, probably for no other reason except that it was usual for kings to take names of good omen, connected with the sun, or the moon, or the stars—in which case a myth, connected with a solar name, would naturally be transferred to its human namesake. In the ancient poetical and proverbial language of Elis, people said ' Selene loves and watches Endymion,' instead of ' it is getting late ' ; ' Selene embraces Endymion,' instead of ' the sun is setting and the moon is rising ' ; ' Selene kisses Endymion into sleep,' instead of ' it is night.' These expressions remained long after their meaning had ceased to be understood ; and as the human mind is generally as anxious for a reason as ready to invent one, a story arose by common consent, and without any personal effort, that Endymion must have been a young lad loved by a young lady, Selene ; and, if children were anxious to know still more, there would always be a grandmother happy to tell them that this young Endymion was the son of the Protogeneia—she half meaning and half not meaning by that

name the Dawn, who gave birth to the sun ;
or of Kalyke, the dark and covering Night.
This name, once touched, would set many
chords vibrating ; three or four different
reasons might be given (as they really were
given by ancient poets) why Endymion fell
into this everlasting sleep, and if any one
of these was alluded to by a popular poet,
it became a mythological fact, repeated by
later poets ; so that Endymion grew at last
almost into a type, no longer of the setting
sun, but of a handsome boy beloved of a
chaste maiden, and therefore a most likely
name for a young prince. Many myths
have thus been transferred to real persons,
by a mere similarity of name, though it
must be admitted that there is no historical
evidence whatsoever that there ever was
a Prince of Elis, called by the name of
Endymion.

Such is the growth of a legend, originally
a mere word, a μύθος, probably one of those
many words which have but a local currency, and lose their value if they are taken
to distant places—words useless for the
daily interchange of thought—spurious coins
in the hands of the many—yet not thrown
away, but preserved as curiosities and ornaments, and deciphered at last, after many
centuries, by the antiquarian. Unfortunately, we do not possess these legends as
they passed originally from mouth to mouth
in villages or mountain castles—legends such

as Grimm has collected in his *Mythology*,
from the language of the poor people in
Germany—not as they were told by the
older members of a family, who spoke a
language half intelligible to themselves and
strange to their children—not as the poet of
a rising city embodied the traditions of his
neighbourhood in a continuous poem, and
gave to them a certain form and permanence.
Unless where Homer has preserved a local
myth, all is arranged as a system, with the
Theogony as its beginning, the *Siege of Troy*
as its centre, and the *Return of the Heroes*
as its end.   But how many parts of Greek
mythology are never mentioned by Homer !
We then come to Hesiod—a moralist and
theologian, and again we find but a small
segment of the mythological language of
Greece.   Thus, our chief sources are the
ancient chroniclers, who took mythology
for history, and used of it only so much as
answered their purpose.   And not even these
are preserved to us, but we only believe
that they formed the sources from which
later writers, such as Apollodorus and the
scholiasts, borrowed their information.   The
first duty of the mythologist is, therefore,
to disentangle this cluster, to remove all
that is systematic, and to reduce each myth
to its primitive unsystematic form.   Much
that is unessential has to be cut away
altogether, and after the rust is removed,
we have to determine first of all, as with

ancient coins, the locality, and, if possible, the age, of each myth, by the character of its workmanship ; and as we arrange ancient medals into gold, silver, and copper coins, we have to distinguish most carefully between the legends of gods, heroes, and men. If, then, we succeed in deciphering the ancient names and legends of Greek or any other mythology, we learn that the past that stands before our eyes, in Greek mythology, has had its present—that there are traces of organic thought in these petrified relics—and that they once formed the surface of the Greek language. The legend of Endymion was present at the time when the people of Elis understood the old saying of the Moon (or Selene) rising under the cover of Night (or in the Latmian cave), to see and admire, in silent love, the beauty of the setting Sun, the sleeper Endymion, the son of Zeus, who granted to him the double boon of eternal sleep and everlasting youth.

Endymion is not the Sun in the divine character of Phoibos Apollon, but a conception of the Sun in his daily course, as rising early from the womb of Dawn,[1] and after a short and brilliant career, setting in the evening, never to return again to this mortal life. Similar conceptions are frequent in Aryan mythology, and the Sun viewed in this light is sometimes represented

[1] [So in Psalm cx. 3, the Messiah has His birth ' from the womb of the morning.']

as divine, yet not immortal—sometimes as living, but sleeping—sometimes as a mortal beloved by a goddess, yet tainted by the fate of humanity. Thus, *Tithonos* being derived from the same root as Titan,[1] expressed originally the idea of the Sun in his daily or yearly character. He also, like Endymion, does not enjoy the full immortality of Zeus and Apollon. Endymion retains his youth, but is doomed to sleep. Tithonos is made immortal, but as Eos forgot to ask for his eternal youth, he pines away as a decrepit old man, in the arms of his ever youthful wife, who loved him when he was young, and is kind to him in his old age. Other traditions, careless about contradictions, or ready to solve them sometimes by the most atrocious expedients, call Tithonos the son of Eos and Kephalos, as Endymion was the son of Protogeneia, the Dawn; and this freedom in handling a myth shows, that at first, a Greek knew what it meant if Eos was said to leave every morning the bed of Tithonos. As long as this expression was understood, I should say that the myth was present; it was past when Tithonos had been changed into a son of Laomedon, a brother of Priamos, a prince of Troy. Then the saying, that Eos left his bed in the morning, became mythical, and had none but a conventional or traditional meaning. Then, as Tithonos

---

[1] Ἀφελῶς δ' ἔλαμψε Τίταν.—*Anakreontea*, 47.

was a prince of Troy, his son, the Ethiopian Memnon, had to take part in the Trojan war. And yet how strange !—even then the old myth seems to float through the dim memory of the poet !—for when Eos weeps for her son, the beautiful Memnon, her tears are called ' morning-dew '—so that the past may be said to have been still half-present.[1]

As we have mentioned Kephalos as the beloved of Eos, and the father of Tithonos, we may add, that Kephalos also, like Tithonos and Endymion, was one of the many names of the Sun. Kephalos, however, was the rising sun—the head of light—an expression frequently used of the sun in different mythologies.[2] In the *Veda*, where the sun is addressed as a horse, the head of the horse is an expression meaning the rising sun. Thus, the poet says—*Rv.* i. 163, 6, ' I have known through my mind thy self

[1] [As an instance of the solidarity of classical myths with those of primitive peoples, this from New Zealand may be compared : ' Up to this time the vast Heaven has still ever remained separated from his spouse the Earth. Yet this mutual love still continues—the soft warm sighs of her loving bosom still ever rise up to him, ascending from the woody mountains and valleys, and men call them mists ; and the vast Heaven, as he mourns through the long nights his separation from his beloved, drops frequent tears upon her bosom, and men seeing these term them dew-drops.'—Sir G. Grey, *Polynesian Mythology*, 1855, p. 15.]

[2] [*E.g.* ' (Sol) caput obscura nitidum ferrugine texit.' —Vergil, *Georgic*, i. 467.

' The mounting sun,
Through thick exhaled fogs his golden head hath run.'
—M. Drayton, *Polyolbion*, Song 13, *sub init.*]

when it was still far—thee, the bird flying up from below the sky ; I saw a head with wings, proceeding on smooth and dustless paths.' The Teutonic nations speak of the sun as the eye of Wuotan, as Hesiod speaks of—

πάντα ἰδὼν Διὸς ὀφθαλμὸς καὶ πάντα νοήσας;

and they also call the sun the face of their god.[1] In the *Veda*, again, the sun is called (i. 115, 1) ' the face of the gods,' or the face of Aditi [the Infinite] (i. 113, 9) ; and it is said that the winds obscure the eye of the sun by showers of rain (v. 59, 5).

A similar idea led the Greeks to form the name of Kephalos ; and if Kephalos is called the son of Herse—the Dew—this meant the same in mythological language, that we should express by the sun rising over dewy fields. What is told of Kephalos is, that he was the husband of Prokris, that he loved her, and that they vowed to be faithful to one another. But Eos also loves Kephalos ; she tells her love, and Kephalos, true to Prokris, does not accept it. Eos, who knows her rival, replies, that he might remain faithful to Prokris, till Prokris had broken her vow. Kephalos accepts the challenge,

[1] Grimm, *Mythologie*, 666. [Eng. trans., 703. We may perhaps compare the Semitic use of *pani*, face, for the manifestation of a deity, *e.g. Peni-el*, ' face of God ' (Gen. xxxii. 30, 31), equivalent to the Babylonian *pâni-îli*, and ' the face (*pen*) of Baal,' a name given to the Carthaginian goddess Tanith. This explains a difficult passage in Hosea xi. 2.]

approaches his wife disguised as a stranger, and gains her love. Prokris, discovering her shame, flies to Kreta. Here Diana gives her a dog and a spear, that never miss their aim, and Prokris returns to Kephalos disguised as a huntsman. While hunting with Kephalos, she is asked by him to give him the dog and the spear. She promises to do so only in return for his love, and when he has assented, she discloses herself, and is again accepted by Kephalos. Yet Prokris fears the charms of Eos—and while jealously watching her husband, she is killed by him unintentionally, by the spear that never misses its aim.

Before we can explain this myth, which, however, is told with many variations by Greek and Latin poets, we must dissect it, and reduce it to its constituent elements.

The first is ' Kephalos loves Prokris.' Prokris we must explain by a reference to Sanskrit, where prush and prish mean, ' to sprinkle,' and are used chiefly with reference to raindrops. For instance, *Rv.* i. 168, 8. ' The lightnings laugh down upon the earth,[1] when the Winds shower forth the rain.'

The same root in the Teutonic languages has taken the sense of ' frost '—and Bopp identifies prush with O. H. G. frus, frigere.

[1] [*Cf.* the Persian *khandah i barq*, ' the laughter of the lightning ' ; and Shelley makes the cloud say, ' I laugh as I pass in thunder.' So Lucretius, ' Æther lumine *ridet*' (iii. 22) ; ' the light of the righteous laugheth.'—Prov. xiii. 9.]

In Greek we must refer to the same root πρώξ, πρωκός, a dewdrop, and also Prŏkris, the dew. Thus, the wife of Kephalos is only a repetition of Herse, her mother—Herse, dew, being derived from Sk. vrish, to sprinkle. The first part of our myth, therefore, means simply, ' the Sun kisses the Morning Dew.'

The second saying is, ' Eos loves Kephalos.' This requires no explanation: it is the old story, repeated a hundred times in Aryan mythology, ' the Dawn loves the Sun.'

The third saying was, ' Prokris is faithless; yet her new lover, though in a different guise, is still the same Kephalos.' This we may interpret as a poetical expression for the rays of the sun being reflected in various colours from the dewdrops—so that Prokris may be said to be kissed by many lovers; yet they are all the same Kephalos, disguised, but at last recognised.

The last saying was, ' Prokris is killed by Kephalos,' *i.e.* the dew is absorbed by the sun. Prokris dies for her love to Kephalos, and he must kill her because he loves her. It is the gradual and inevitable absorption of the dew by the glowing rays of the sun which is expressed, with so much truth, by the unerring shaft of Kephalos thrown unintentionally at Prokris hidden in the thicket of the forest.[1]

[1] ' La rugiada
Pugna col sole.'—Dante, *Purgatorio*, 1, 121.

H

We have only to put these four sayings together, and every poet will at once tell us the story of the love and jealousy of Kephalos, Prokris, and Eos. If anything was wanted to confirm the solar nature of Kephalos, we might point out how the first meeting of Kephalos and Prokris takes place on Mount Hymettos, and how Kephalos throws himself afterwards, in despair, into the sea, from the Leukadian mountains. Now, the whole myth belongs to Attika, and here the sun would rise, during the greater part of the year, over Mount Hymettos like a brilliant head. A straight line from this, the most eastern point, to the most western headland of Greece, carries us to the Leukadian promontory—and here Kephalos might well be said to have drowned his sorrows in the waves of the ocean.[1]

[1] [The Leukadian rock faces the entrance to the under-world, 'the portals of the sun,' when he sinks into the darkness of the west (Homer, *Odyssey*, xxiv. 11, 12). It was the leaping-off place for despairing lovers and death-doomed criminals (Ovid, *Fasti*, v. 630; *Hesiod*, xv. 179). They were conceived as following the sun in his descent as—

' A god gigantic, habited in gold,
Stepping from off a mount into the sea.'

(C. Wells).

Similarly the New Zealanders regard Reinga, at the north end of the islands, as the leaping-off place which gives entrance to their Hades, 'the great Mother-Night' (R. Taylor, *New Zealand*, 148. 231). In Mangaia the point of departure when they leap into the sea for spirit-land, Avaiki, faces the setting sun (W. W. Gill, *Myths and Songs of S. Pacific*, 159). At the west point of Upolu is the leaping-stone, giving a

Another magnificent sunset looms in the myth of the death of Herakles. His two-fold character as a god, and as a hero, is acknowledged even by Herodotos—and some of his epithets are sufficient to indicate his solar character, though perhaps no name has been made the vehicle of so many mythological and historical, physical and moral stories, as that of Herakles. Names which he shaies with Apollo and Zeus are Δαφνηφόρος, Ἀλεξίκακος, Μάντις, Ἰδαῖος, Ὀλύμπιος, Παγγενέτωρ.

Now, in his last journey, Herakles also, like Kephalos, proceeds from east to west. He is performing his sacrifice to Zeus, on the Kenaeon promontory of Euboea, when Deianeira sends him the fatal garment. He then throws Lichas into the sea—who is transformed into the Lichadian islands. From thence Herakles crosses over to Trachys, and then to Mount Oeta, where his pile is raised, and the hero is burnt, rising through the clouds to the seat of the immortal goas—himself henceforth immortal and wedded to Hebe, the goddess of youth. The coat which Deianeira sends to the solar hero is an expression frequently used in

direct route to Fāfā (Hades).—J. B. Stair, *Old Samoa*, 219. The old Norsemen cast themselves from the Val-halla cliff into Odin's Pond (the sea) to gain immortality.—C. Elton, *Origins of English History*, 91-2. See also R. Brown, *Essays*, 257-60. So Cape Raz, the extreme western point of Armorica, is held by the Bretons to be the place of departure of souls for the under-world (Procopius, Claudian, Villemarqué).]

other mythologies ; it is the coat which in the *Veda*, ' the mothers weave for their bright son '—the clouds which rise from the waters and surround the sun like a dark raiment.   Herakles tries to tear it off ; his fierce splendour breaks through the thickening gloom—but fiery mists embrace him, and are mingled with the parting rays of the sun, and the dying hero is seen through the scattered clouds of the sky, tearing his own body to pieces, till at last his bright body is consumed in a general conflagration, his last-beloved being Iole—perhaps the violet-coloured evening clouds—a word which, as it reminds us also of ἰός, poison (though the ι is long), may perhaps have originated the myth of a poisoned garment.

In these legends the Greek language supplies almost all that is necessary in order to render these strange stories intelligible and rational, though the later Greeks—I mean Homer and Hesiod, had certainly in most cases no suspicion of the original import of their own traditions.   But as there are Greek words which find no explanation in Greek, and which, without a reference to Sanskrit and the other cognate dialects, would have for ever remained to the philologist mere sounds with a conventional meaning, there are also names of gods and heroes inexplicable, from a Greek point of view, and which cannot be made to disclose their primitive character, unless confronted with contemporary witnesses from India, Persia, Italy, or Germany. Another myth of the dawn will best explain this:—

Ahan in Sanskrit is a name of the day, and is said to stand for dahan, like a*s*ru, tear, for da*s*ru, Greek δάκρυ. Whether we have to admit an actual loss of this initial d, or whether the d is to be considered rather as a secondary letter, by which the root ah was individualised to dah, is a question ·which does not concern us at present. In Sanskrit we have the root dah, which means, to burn, and from which a name of the day might have been formed in the same manner as dyu—day, is formed from dyu, to be brilliant. Nor does it concern us here, whether the Gothic *dags*, day, is the same word or not. According to Grimm's law, *daha*, in Sanskrit, should in Gothic appear as *taga*, and not as *daga*.[1] However, there are several of the old common Aryan names in which Grimm's law is violated, and Bopp seems inclined to consider daga and daha identical in origin. Certain it is that the same root from which the Teutonic words for *day* are formed, has also given rise to the name for dawn. In German we say ' der Morgen *tagt*,' and in Old English day was *dawe*, while to dawn was in Anglo-Saxon *dagian*. Now, in the *Veda*, one of

[1] [M. Müller in his later writings postulated *dhah* as a mediating form between *dah* and *daga*.]

the names of the dawn is Ahanâ. It occurs
only once, *Rv.* i. 123, 4.

> Grihám griham Ahanâ' yâti *ákkha*
> Divédive ádhi nâ'ma dádhânâ
> Sísâsantí Dyotanâ' *sásvat* â' agât
> A'gram agram ít bha*g*ate vásûnâm.

' Ahanâ (the dawn) comes near to every house
—she who makes every day to be known.
' Dyotanâ (the dawn), the active maiden,
comes back for evermore—she enjoys always
the first of all goods.'

We have already seen the Dawn in various
relations to the Sun, but not yet as the
beloved of the Sun, flying before her lover,
and destroyed by his embrace. This, however, was a very familiar expression in the
old mythological language of the Aryans.
The Dawn has died in the arms of the Sun,
or the Dawn is flying before the Sun, or the
Sun has shattered the car of the Dawn,
were expressions meaning simply, the sun
has risen—the dawn is gone. Thus, we read
in the *Rv.* iv. 30, in a hymn celebrating the
achievements of Indra, the chief solar deity
of the *Veda*—

' And this strong and manly deed also thou
hast performed, O Indra, that thou struckest
the daughter of Dyaus (the Dawn), a woman
difficult to vanquish.
' Yes, even the daughter of Dyaus, the magnified, the Dawn, thou, O Indra, a great hero,
hast ground to pieces.
' The Dawn rushed off from her crushed

car, fearing that Indra, the bull, might strike her.

' This her car lay there well ground to pieces ; she went far away.'

In this case, Indra behaves rather unceremoniously to the daughter of the sky ; but, in other places, she is loved by all the bright gods of heaven, not excluding her own father. The Sun, it is said, *Rv.* i. 115, 2, follows her from behind, as a man follows a woman. ' She, the Dawn, whose cart is drawn by white horses, is carried away in triumph by the two A*s*vins,'—as the Leukippides are carried off by the Dioskuroi.[1]

If now we translate, or rather transliterate, *Dahaná* into Greek, Daphne stands before us, and her whole history is intelligible. Daphne is ' young, and beautiful—Apollo loves her—she flies before him, and dies as he embraces her with his brilliant rays.' Or, as another poet of the *Veda* (x. 189), expresses it, ' The Dawn comes near to him —she expires as soon as he begins to breathe —the mighty one irradiates the sky.' Any one who has eyes to see and a heart to feel with nature like the poets of old, may still see Daphne and Apollo—the dawn rushing and trembling through the sky, and fading

---

[1] [For the identification of the Asvins with the Dioskuroi, see J. Rendel Harris, *The Dioscuri in the Christian Legends*, 12, 26, 36, and *Cult of the Heavenly Twins*, 51 ; M. Müller, *Contributions to Mythology*, 535-42 ; Whitney, *Oriental and Linguistic Studies*, 38.]

away at the sudden approach of the bright sun. The metamorphosis of Daphne into a laurel-tree is a continuation of the myth of peculiarly Greek growth. Daphne, in Greek, meant no longer the dawn, but it had become the name of the laurel. Hence the tree Daphne was considered sacred to the lover of Daphne, the dawn, and Daphne herself was fabled to have been changed into a tree when praying to her mother to protect her from the violence of Apollo.[1]

Without the help of the *Veda*, the name of Daphne and the legend attached to her, would have remained unintelligible, for the later Sanskrit supplies no key to this name. This shows the value of the *Veda* for the purpose of comparative mythology, a science which, without the *Veda*, would have remained mere guesswork, without fixed principles and without a safe basis.

In order to show in how many different ways the same idea may be expressed mythologically, I have confined myself to the

---

[1] Cf. *Rv.* iv. 30.

[Δάφνη (by-forms δαύχνη and δαυχμός) was understood to be the inflammable wood, and so radically akin to the fiery dawn. M. Müller was not aware of the very interesting parallel in Ancient Egyptian, where '*beq* represents the brightness of the dawn' and also 'the olive tree' (from *beq*, bright)—Renouf, *Trans. Soc. Bib. Archæology*, viii. 219 ; *Proc. S. B. A.*, xiv. 219 ; Theophrastus says that the fire-drill was made of laurel (no doubt because a wood that ignites easily (*Hist. Plantarum*, v. 9, in O. Peschel, *Races of Men*, 144). See further in M. Müller, *Science of Language*, eighth ed., ii. 548–49.]

names of the Dawn. The dawn is really
one of the richest sources of Aryan mythology ; and another class of legends, embodying the strife between winter and summer,
the return of spring, the revival of nature,
is in most languages but a reflection and
amplification of the more ancient stories
telling of the strife between night and day,
the return of the morn, and the revival
of the whole world. The stories, again, of
solar heroes fighting through a thunder-
storm against the powers of darkness, are
borrowed from the same source ; and the
cows, so frequently alluded to in the *Veda*,
as carried off by V*r*itra and brought back
by Indra, are in reality the same bright
cows which the Dawn drives out every
morning to their pasture-ground—the clouds
—which, from their heavy udders, send
down refreshing and fertilising rain or dew
upon the parched earth. There is no sight
in nature more elevating than the dawn
even to us, whom philosophy has taught that
' nil admirari ' is the highest wisdom. Yet in
ancient times the power of admiring was the
greatest blessing bestowed on mankind ; and
when could man have admired more intensely, when could his heart have been more
gladdened and overpowered with joy than at
the approach of
   ' the Lord of light,
  Of life, of love, and gladness ! '
The darkness of night fills the human heart

with despondency and awe, and a feeling of fear and anguish sets every nerve trembling. There is man like a forlorn child fixing his eye with breathless anxiety upon the East, the womb of day, where the light of the world has flamed up so many times before. As the father waits the birth of his child, so the poet watches the dark heaving night who is to bring forth her bright son, the sun of the day. The doors of heaven seem slowly to open, and what are called the bright flocks of the Dawn step out of the dark stable, returning to their wonted pastures. Who has not seen the gradual advance of this radiant procession—the heaven like a distant sea tossing its golden waves—when the first rays shoot forth like brilliant horses racing round the whole course of the horizon—when the clouds begin to colour up, each shedding her own radiance over her more distant sisters ! Not only the East, but the West, and the South, and the North, the whole temple of heaven is illuminated, and the pious worshipper lights in response his own small light on the altar of the hearth, and stammers words which express but faintly the joy that is in nature and in the human heart—

' Rise ! our life, our spirit is come back ! the darkness is gone, the light approaches ! '

If the people of antiquity called these eternal lights of heaven their gods, their bright ones (deva), the Dawn was the first-born among all the gods—Protogeneia—dearest to man, and always young and fresh. But if not raised to an immortal state, if only admired as a kind being, awakening every morning the children of man, her life would seem to be short. She soon fades away, and dies when the fountain-head of light rises in naked splendour, and sends his first swift glance through the vault of heaven. We cannot realise that sentiment with which the eye of antiquity dwelt on these sights of nature. To us all is law, order, necessity. We calculate the refractory power of the atmosphere, we measure the possible length of the dawn in every climate, and the rising of the sun is to us no greater surprise than that two and two make four. But if we could believe again, that there was in the sun a being like our own, that in the dawn there was a soul open to human sympathy—if we could bring ourselves to look for a moment upon these powers as personal, free, and adorable, how different would be our feelings at the blush of day ! That Titanic assurance with which we say, the sun *must* rise, was unknown to the early worshippers of nature, or if they also began to feel the regularity with which the sun and the other stars perform their daily labour, they still thought of free beings kept in temporary servitude, chained for a time, and bound to obey a higher will, but sure to rise, like Herakles, to a higher glory at the end of their labours. It seems to us childish when we read in the *Veda* such expressions as, 'Will the Sun rise?' 'Will our old friend, the Dawn, come back again?' 'Will the powers of darkness be conquered by the God of Light?' And when the Sun rose, they wondered how, but just born, he was so mighty, and strangled, as it were, in his cradle, the serpents of the night. They asked how he could walk along the sky? why there was no dust on his road? why he did not fall backward? But at last they greeted him like a poet of our own time—

'Hail, orient Conqueror of gloomy Night!'

and the human eye felt that it could not bear the brilliant majesty of Him whom they call 'the Life, the Breath, the brilliant Lord and Father.'

Thus sunrise was the revelation of nature, awakening in the human mind that feeling of dependence, of helplessness, of hope, of joy and faith in higher powers, which is the source of all wisdom, the spring of all religion. But if sunrise inspired the first prayers, called forth the first sacrificial flames, sunset was the other time when, again, the whole frame of man would tremble. The shadows of night approach, the irresistible power of sleep grasps man in the midst of his pleasures, his friends depart, and in his loneliness his thoughts turn again to higher powers. When the day departs, the poet bewails the untimely death of his bright friend, nay, he sees in his short career the likeness of his own life. Perhaps, when he has fallen asleep, his sun may never rise again, and thus the place to which the setting sun withdraws in the far West rises before his mind as the abode where he himself would go after death, where 'his fathers went before him,' and where all the wise and the pious rejoice in a 'new life with Yama and Varu*n*a,' Or he might look upon the sun, not as a short-lived hero, but as young, unchanging, and always the same, while generations after generations of mortal men were passing away. And hence, by the mere force of contrast, the first intimation of beings which do not wither and decay—of immortals, of immortality ! Then the poet would implore the immortal sun to come again, to vouchsafe to the sleeper a new morning. The god of day would become the god of time, of life and death. Again, the evening twilight, the sister of the dawn, repeating, though with a more sombre light, the wonders of the morning, how many feelings must it have roused in the musing poet— how many poems must it have elicited in the living language of ancient times ! Was it the dawn that came again to give a last embrace to him who had parted from her in the morning ? Was she the immortal, the always returning goddess, and he the mortal, the daily dying sun ? Or was she the mortal, bidding a last farewell to her immortal lover, burnt, as it were, on the same pile which would consume her, while he would rise to the seat of the gods ?

Let us express these simple scenes in ancient language, and we shall find ourselves surrounded on every side by mythology full of contradictions and incongruities, the same being represented as mortal or immortal, as man or woman, as the poetical eye of man shifts its point of view, and gives its own colour to the mysterious play of nature.

One of the myths of the *Veda* which expresses this correlation of the Dawn and the Sun, this love between the Immortal and the Mortal, and the identity of the Morning Dawn and the Evening Twilight, is the story of Urvasî and Purûravas. The two names, Urvasî and Purûravas, are to the Hindu mere proper names, and even in the *Veda* their original meaning has almost entirely faded away. There is a dialogue in the *Rigveda* between Urvasî and Purûravas, where both appear personified in the same manner as in the play of *Kalidâsa*. The first point, therefore, which we have to prove is that Urvasî was originally an appellation, and meant dawn.

The etymology of Urvasî is difficult. It

cannot be derived from urva by means of the suffix sa,[1] as Dr. Kuhn proposes, because there is no such word as *urva*, and because derivatives in sa, like romasá, yuvasá, &c., have the accent on the last syllable. I therefore accept the common Indian explanation by which this name is derived from *uru*, wide (εὐρυ), and a root, as, to pervade, and thus compare uru-así, with another frequent epithet of the Dawn, urûkî, the feminine of uru-ak, far-going. It was certainly one of the most striking features, and one by which the Dawn was distinguished from all the other dwellers in the heavens, that she occupies the wide expanse of the sky, and that her horses ride, as it were, with the swiftness of thought round the whole horizon. Hence we find that names beginning with *uru* in Sanskrit, and with εὐρυ in Greek, are almost invariably old mythological names of the Dawn or the Twilight. The Earth also, it is true, claims this epithet, but in different combinations from those which apply to the bright goddess. Names of the Dawn are Euryphaessa, the mother of Helios, Eurykyde or Eurypyle, the daughter of Endymion, Eurymede, the wife of Glaukos, Eurynome, the mother of the Charites, and Eurydike, the wife of Orpheus, whose character as an ancient god will be discussed hereafter. In the *Veda* the name of Ushas

[1] *Pânini*, v. 2, 100.

or Eos, is hardly ever mentioned without some allusion to her far and wide-spreading splendour ; such as ' urviyâ vibhâti,' she shines wide ; ' urviyâ vikâkshe,' she looks far and wide ; ' varîyasî,' the widest,[1] whereas the light of the Sun is not represented as wide-stretching, but rather as far-darting.

But there are other indications besides the mere name of Urvasî, which lead us to suppose that she was originally the goddess of the dawn. Vasishtha, though best known as the name of one of the chief poets of the *Veda*, is the superlative of vasu, bright, and as such also a name of the Sun. Thus it happens that expressions which apply properly to the sun only, were transferred to the ancient poet. He is called the son of Mitra and Varuna, night and day, an expression which has a meaning only with regard to Vasishtha, the sun ; and as the sun is frequently called the offspring of the dawn, Vasishtha, the poet, is said to owe his birth to Urvasî. (*Rv.* vii. 33, 11.) The

[1] The name which approaches nearest to Urvasî in Greek might seem to be *Europe*, because the palatal *s* is occasionally represented by a Greek π, as asva = ἵππος. The only difficulty is the long ω in Greek, otherwise Europe, carried away by the white bull (vrisha, man, bull, stallion, in the *Veda* a frequent appellation of the sun, and sveta, white, applied to the same deity), carried away on his back (the dawn being frequently represented as at the back of the sun, *cf.* Eurydike) ; again carried to a distant cave (the gloaming of the evening) ; and mother of *Apollo*, the god of daylight, or of *Minos* (Manu, a mortal Zeus), would well agree with the goddess of the dawn.

peculiarity of his birth reminds us strongly of the birth of Aphrodite, as told by Hesiod.

Again, we find that in the few passages where the name of Urvaʂî occurs in the *Rigveda,* the same attributes and actions are ascribed to her which usually belong to Ushas, the Dawn.

It is frequently said of Ushas, that she prolongs the life of man, and the same is said of Urvaʂî. (*Rv.* iv. 2, 18 ; v. 41, 19 ; x. 95, 10.) In one passage Urvaʂî is even used as a plural, in the sense of many dawns or days increasing the life of man, which shows that the appellative power of the word was not yet quite forgotten. Again, she is called antarikshaprâ, filling the air, a usual epithet of the sun, brihaddivâ, with mighty splendour, all indicating the bright presence of the dawn. However, the best proof that Urvaʂî was the dawn is the legend told of her and her love to Purûravas, a story that is true only of the Sun and the Dawn. That *Purûravas* is an appropriate name of a solar hero requires hardly any proof. Purûravas meant the same as πολυδευκης, 'endowed with much light'; for though *rava* is generally used of sound, yet the root *ru,* which means originally to cry, is also applied to colour,[1] in the sense

[1] Thus it is said (*Rv.* vi. 3, 6) the fire cries with light (ʂokishâ) rarapitî ; the two Spartan Charites are called Κλητά and Φαεννά, *i.e.* Clara, clear-sounding and clear-shining. Of the rising sun it is said in the *Veda* [ix. 74, 1] ' the child cries.' [*Cf.* Sanskrit *ravi,*

I

of a loud or crying colour, *i.e.* red (cf. *rudhira*,
ἐρυθρός, *ruber*, *rufus*, Lith. *rauda*, O.H.G. *rôt*).
Besides, Purûravas calls himself Vasish*tha*,
which, as we know, is a name of the Sun ;
and if he is called Ai*da*, the son of Id*â*, the
same name is elsewhere (*Rv.* iii. 29, 3) given
to Agni, the fire.

Now the story, in its most ancient form,
is found in the Brâhm*ana* of the *Yagurveda*.
There we read :

' Urvasî, a kind of fairy, fell in love with
Purûravas, the son of Id*â*, and when she met
him, she said : ' Embrace me three times a-day,
but never against my will, and let me never
see you without your royal garments.' In this
manner she lived with him a long time. Then
her former friends, the Gandharvas, said : ' This
Urvasî has now dwelt a long time among mortals ;
let us see that she come back.' Now, there
was a ewe, with two lambs, tied to the couch
of Urvasî and Purûravas, and the Gandharvas
stole one of them. Urvasî said : ' They take
away my darling, as if I lived in a land where
there is no hero and no man.' They stole the
second, and she upbraided her husband again.
Then Purûravas looked and said : ' How can
that be a land without heroes or men where I
am ? ' And, naked, he sprang up ; he thought it
too long to put on his dress. Then the Gandharvas sent a flash of lightning, and Urvasî saw

---

' roarer,' ' shiner,' the sun. I have brought together
a large number of instances of the interchange of
sound and light words, to illustrate the ' silence ' of
the sun in Joshua x. 12, in my book *A Misunderstood
Miracle*, 1887, pp. 16–31, 81–88. See also some good
observations in L. Noire, *M. Müller and the Philosophy
of Language*, 86, 87.]

her husband naked as by daylight. Then she vanished; 'I come back,' she said—and went. Then he bewailed his vanished love in bitter grief; and went near Kurukshetra. There is a lake there, called Anyata*h*plaksha, full of lotus flowers, and while the king walked along its border, the fairies were playing there in the water, in the shape of birds. And Urvasî discovered him, and said: 'That is the man with whom I dwelt so long.' Then her friends said: 'Let us appear to him.' She agreed, and they appeared before him. Then the king recognised her and said: 'Lo! my wife! stay, thou cruel in mind! let us now exchange some words! Our secrets, if they are not told now, will not bring us luck on any later day.' She replied: 'What shall I do with thy speech? I am gone like the first of the dawns. Purûravas, go home again! I am hard to be caught, like the wind.' He said, in despair: 'Then may thy former friend now fall down, never to rise again; may he go far, far away! May he lie down on the threshold of death, and may rabid wolves there devour him!' She replied: 'Purûravas, do not die! do not fall down! may no evil wolves devour thee! there is no friendship with women, their hearts are the hearts of wolves. When I walked among mortals under a different form—when I dwelt with thee, many nights during four autumns, I ate once a day a small piece of butter—and even now I feel pleasure from it.' Thus, at last, her heart melted, and she said: 'Come to me the last night of the year, and thou shalt be with me for one night, and a son will be born to thee.' He went the last night of the year to the golden seats, and while he was alone, he was told to go up, and then they sent Urvasî to him. Then she said: 'The Gandharvas will to-morrow grant thee a wish ; choose ! ' He said : ' Choose thou for me.' She replied : ' Say to them, Let me be one of you.' Early the next morn, the Gandharvas gave him his choice ; but when he said ' Let me be one of you,' they said : ' That kind of sacred fire is not yet known to man, by which he could perform a sacrifice, and become one of ourselves.' They then initiated Purûravas in the mysteries of a certain sacrifice, and when he had performed it, he became himself one of the Gandharvas.'

This is the simple story, told in the Brâhma*n*a, in order to show the importance of a peculiar rite ; this rite of kindling the fire by friction being represented as the one by which Purûravas obtained immortality. The verses quoted in the story are taken from the *Rigveda*, where we find, in the last book, together with many strange relics of popular poetry, a dialogue between the two lovers. It consists of seventeen verses, while the author of the Brâhma*n*a knew only fifteen. But in one of the verses which he quotes, Urva*s*î says, ' I am gone for ever, like the first of the dawns,' which shows a strange glimmering of the old myth in the mind of the poet, and reminds us of the tears which the mother of Memnon shed over the corpse of her son, and which even by later poets are called morning dew. Again, in the fourth verse, Urva*s*î addressing herself, says : ' This person (that is to say I) when she was wedded to him, O Dawn ! she went to his house, and was embraced by him day and night.' Again she tells Purûravas that he was created by the gods in order to stay the powers of darkness (dasyuhatyâya), a task invariably ascribed to Indra and other solar beings. Even the names of the companions of Urvasî point to the dawn, and Purûravas says:

' When I, the mortal, threw my arms around those flighty immortals, they trembled away from me like a trembling doe, like horses that kick against the cart.'

No goddess is so frequently called the friend of man as the Dawn. ' She goes to every house ' (i. 123, 4) ; ' she thinks of the dwelling of man ' (i. 123, 1) ; ' she does not despise the small or the great ' (i. 124, 6) ; ' she brings wealth ' (i. 48, 1) ; ' she is always the same, immortal, divine ' (i. 124, 4 ; i. 123, 8) ; ' she does not grow old ' (i. 113, 15) ; ' she is the young goddess, but she makes man grow old ' (i. 92, 11). Thus Purûravas called Urvasî ' the immortal among the mortals ' ; and, in his last verse, he addressed his beloved in the following words :

' I, the brightest Sun, I hold Urvasî, her who fills the air (with light), who spreads the sky. May the blessing of thy kind deed be upon thee ! Come back, the heart burns me.'

Then the poet says :

' Thus the gods spake to thee, O son of Idâ : in order that thou, bound to death, mayest grow to be this (immortal), thy race should worship the gods with oblations! Then thou also wilt rejoice in heaven.'

We must certainly admit, that even in the *Veda*, the poets were as ignorant of the original meaning of Urvaṣî and Purûravas as Homer was of Tithonos, if not of Eos. To them they were heroes, indefinite beings, men yet not men, gods yet not gods. But to us, though placed at a much greater distance, they disclose their true meaning. As Wordsworth says :

'Not unrejoiced, I see thee climb the sky
In naked splendour, clear from mist and haze '—

Antiquity spoke of the naked sun, and of the chaste dawn hiding her face when she had seen her husband. Yet she says she will come again. And after the sun has travelled through the world in search of his beloved, when he comes to the threshold of death and is going to end his solitary life, she appears again in the gloaming, the same as the dawn—as Eos in Homer begins and ends the day—and she carries him away to the golden seats of the immortals.[1]

[1] *Od.* v. 390, ἀλλ' ὅτε δὴ τρίτον ἦμαρ ἐϋπλόκαμος τέλεσ' ἠώς.
[Quite in the primitive Aryan spirit is Tennyson's stanza :—

'The dim red morn had died, her journey done,
    And with dead lips smiled at the twilight plain,
Half-fall'n across the threshold of the sun,
    Never to rise again.'
                    —*Dream of Fair Women.*]

I have selected this myth chiefly in order to show how ancient poetry is only the faint echo of ancient language, and how it was the simple story of nature which inspired the early poet, and held before his mind that deep mirror in which he might see reflected the passions of his own soul. For the heart of man, as long as it knows but its own bitterness, is silent and sullen. It does not tell its love and its loss. There may be a mute poetry in solitary grief, but *Mnemosyne*, the musing goddess of recollection, is not a muse herself, though she is the mother of the muses.[1] It is the sympathy with the grief of others which first gives utterance to the poet's grief, and opens the lips of a silent despair. And if his pain was too deep and too sacred, if he could not compare it with the suffering of any other human heart, the ancient poet had still the heart of nature to commune with, and in her silent suffering he saw a noble likeness of what he felt and suffered within himself. When, after a dark night,

[1] [So Milton contemplated 'a work not to be raised . . . by the invocation of Dame Memory and her siren daughters.'—*Pamphlet*, No. 4, 1641. Musa (Μοῦσα) is 'the deviser,' from the root *man*, to think, whence also *me-min-i*, I mind or remember. M. Müller evidently in the above passage considered Muse to be connected with the verb 'to muse' (so Newman, Coleridge, Patmore). To *muse*, however, is *faire la muse*, to hold one's *muse* or *muzzle* (*musel*) in the air, as a stag does when it sniffs the air in open-mouthed expectation. See my *Folk and their Wordlore*, 147–49.]

the light of the day returned, he thought of his own light that would never rise again. When he saw the Sun kissing the Dawn, he dreamt of days and joys gone for ever. And when the Dawn trembled, and grew pale, and departed, and when the Sun seemed to look for her, and to lose her the more his brilliant eye sought her, an image would rise in his mind, and he would remember his own fate and yet forget it, while telling in measured words the love and loss of the Sun.   Such was the origin of poetry. Nor was the evening without its charms. And when, at the end of a dreary day, the Sun seemed to die away in the far West, still looking for his Eastern bride, and suddenly the heavens opened, and the image of the Dawn rose again, her beauty deepened by a gloaming sadness—would not the poet gaze till the last ray had vanished, and would not the last vanishing ray linger in his heart, and kindle there a hope of another life, where he would find again what he had loved and lost ?

> ' There is a radiant, though a short-lived flame,
> That burns for poets in the dawning east ;
> And oft my soul has kindled at the same,
> When the captivity of sleep had ceased.'
> [—Wordsworth, *Thanksgiving Ode*, 1816.]

There is much suffering in nature to those who have eyes for silent grief, and it is this tragedy—the tragedy of nature—which is the lifespring of all the tragedies of the ancient world. The idea of a young hero, whether he is called Baldr, or Sigurðr, or Sîfrit, or Achilles, or Meleager, or Kephalos, dying in the fulness of youth, a story so frequently told, localised, individualised, was first suggested by the Sun, dying in all his youthful vigour either at the end of a day, struck by the powers of darkness, or at the end of the sunny season, stung by the thorn of winter. Again, that fatal spell by which these sunny heroes must leave their first love, become unfaithful to her or she to them, was borrowed from nature. The fate of these solar heroes was inevitable, and it was their lot to die by the hand or by the unwilling treachery of their nearest friends or relatives. The Sun forsakes the Dawn, and dies at the end of the day, according to an inexorable fate, and bewailed by the whole of nature. Or the Sun is the Sun of Spring, who woos the Earth, and then forsakes his bride and grows cold, and is killed at last by the thorn of Winter. It is an old story, but it is for ever new in the mythology and the legends of the ancient world. Thus Baldr, in the Scandinavian *Edda*, the divine prototype of Sigurðr and Sîfrit, is beloved by the whole world. Gods and men, the whole of nature, all that grows and lives, had sworn to his mother not to hurt the bright hero. The mistletoe alone, that does not grow on the earth, but on trees, had been forgotten, and with it Baldr is killed at the winter solstice.

'So on the floor lay Balder, dead ; and round
Lay thickly strewn, swords, axes, darts, and
    spears,
Which all the gods in sport had idly thrown
At Balder, whom no weapon pierced or clove :
But in his breast stood fixt the fatal bough
Of mistletoe, which Lok, the accuser, gave
To Hoder, and unwitting Hoder threw :
'Gainst that alone had Balder's life no charm.'

Thus Isfendiyar, in the Persian epic, cannot be wounded by any weapon, yet it is his fate to be killed by a thorn, which, as an arrow, is thrown into his eye by Rustem. Rustem, again, can only be killed by his brother ; Herakles, by the mistaken kindness of his wife ; Sîfrit, by the anxious solicitude of Kriemhilt, or by the jealousy of Brunhilt, whom he had forsaken. He is vulnerable in one spot only, like Achilles, and it is there where Hagene (the thorn) strikes him. All these are fragments of solar myths. The whole of nature was divided into two realms—the one dark, cold, wintry, and deathlike, the other bright, warm, vernal, and full of life. Sigurðr, as the solar hero is called in the *Edda*, the descendant of Odin, slays the serpent Fafnir, and conquers the treasure on which Andvari, the dwarf, had pronounced his curse. This is the treasure of the Niflungar, the treasure of the earth which the nebulous powers of winter and darkness had carried away like robbers. The vernal sun wins it back, and like Demeter, rich in the possession of her restored daughter, the earth becomes rich again with all the treasures of spring. He then, according to the *Edda*, delivers Brynhildr, who had been doomed to a magic sleep after being wounded with a thorn by Odin, but who is now, like the spring after the sleep of winter, brought back to new life by the love of Sigurdr. But he, the lord of the treasure (vasupati) is driven onward by his fate. He plights his troth to Brynhildr, and gives her the fatal ring he had taken from the treasure. But he must leave her, and when he arrives at the castle of Gunnar, Gunnar's wife, Grimhildr, makes him forget Brynhildr, and he marries her daughter, Gudrun. Already his course begins to decline. He is bound to Gunnar, nay, he must conquer for him his former bride, Brynhildr, whom Gunnar now marries. Gunnar Gjukason seems to signify darkness, and thus we see that the awakening and budding spring is gone, carried away by Gunnar, like Proserpina by Pluto ; like Sîta by Râvana, Gudrun, the daughter of Grimhildr, and sometimes herself called Grimhildr, whether the latter name meant summer (*cf.* gharma in Sanskrit), or the earth and nature in the latter part of the year, is a sister of the dark Gunnar, and though now married to the bright Sigurdr, she belongs herself to the nebulous regions. Gunnar, who has forced Sigurđr to yield him Brynhilđr, is now planning the death of his kinsman, because Brynhilđr has discovered in Sigurđr her former lover, and must have her revenge. Högni dissuades his brother, Gunnar, from the murder, but at last the third brother, Höđr, stabs Sigurđr while he is asleep at the winter solstice. Brynhilđr has always loved him, and when her hero is killed she distributes the treasure, and is burnt, like Nanna, on the same pile with Sigurđr, a sword being placed between the two lovers. Guđrun also bewails the death of her husband, but she forgets him, and marries Atli, the brother of Brynhilđr. Atli now claims the treasure from Gunnar and Högni, by right of his wife, and when they refuse to give it up, he invites them to his house, and makes them prisoners. Gunnar still refuses to reveal the spot where the treasure is buried till he see the heart of Högni, his brother. A heart is brought him, but it quivers, and he says, ' This is not the heart of my brother.' The real heart of Högni is brought at last, and Gunnar says, ' Now I alone know where the treasure lies, and the Rhine shall rather have it than I will give it up to thee.' He is then bound by Atli, and thrown among serpents. But even the serpents he charms by playing on the harp with his teeth, till at last one viper crawls up to him, and kills him.

How much has this myth been changed if we now read the story of the Nibelunge as it was written down at the end of the twelfth century in Germany. All the heroes are Christians, and have been identified with historical persons of the fourth, fifth, and sixth centuries. Gunther is localised in Burgundy, where we know that, in 435, a Gundicarius or Gundaharius happened to be a real king, the same who, according to Cassiodorus, was vanquished first by Aetius, and afterwards by the Huns of Attila. Hence Atli, the brother of Brynhildr, and the second husband of Gudrun (or Kriemhilt), is identified with Attila, the king of the Huns (453) ; nay, even the brother of Attila, Bleda, is brought in as Blödelin, the first who attacked the Burgundians, and was killed by Dankwart. Other historical persons were drawn into the vortex of the popular story, persons for whom there is no precedent at all in the Edda. Thus we find in the Nibelunge Dietrich von Bern, who is no other but Theodoric the Great (455–525), who conquered Odoacer in the battle of Ravenna (the famous Rabenschlacht), and lived at Verona, in German, Bern. Irenfried, again, the Landgrave of Thuringia, in the poem has been discovered to be Hermanfried, the King of Thuringia, married to Amalaberg, the niece of Theodoric. The most extraordinary coincidence, however, is that by which Sigurđr, the lover of Brynhilđr, has been identified with Siegbert, King of Austrasia from 561 to 575, who was actually married to the famous Brunehault, who actually defeated the Huns, and was actually murdered under the most tragical circumstances by Fredegond, the mistress of his brother Chilperic. This coincidence between myth and history is so great, that it has induced some euhemeristic critics to derive the whole legend of the Nibelunge from Austrasian history, and to make the murder of Siegbert by Brunehault the basis of the murder of Sîfrit or Sigurđr by Brynhilđr. Fortunately, it is easier to answer these German than the old Greek euhemerists, for we find in contemporary history that Jornandes, who wrote his history at least twenty years before the death of the Austrasian Siegbert, knew already the daughter of the mythic Sigurđr, Swanhild, who was born, according to the *Edda*, after the murder of his father, and afterwards killed by Jörmunrekr, whom the poem has again historicised in Hermanicus, a Gothic king of the fourth century.

Let us now apply to the Greek myths what we have learned from the gradual growth of the German myth. There are evidently historical facts round which the myth of Herakles has crystallised, only we cannot substantiate them so clearly as in the myth of the Nibelunge, because we have there no contemporaneous historical documents. Yet as the chief Herakles is represented as belonging to the royal family of Argos, there may have been a Herakles, perhaps the son of a king, called Amphitryo, whose descendants, after a temporary exile, reconquered that part of Greece which had formerly been under the sway of Herakles. The traditions of the miraculous birth, of many of his heroic adventures, and of his death, were as little based on historical facts as the legends of Sîfrit. In Herakles killing the Chimæra and similar monsters, we see the reflected image of the Delphian Apollo killing the worm, or of Zeus, the god of the brilliant sky, with whom Hercules shares in common the names of Idaeos, Olympios, and Pangenetor. As the myth of Sigurđr and Gunnar throws its last broken rays on the kings of Burgundy, and on Attila and Theodoric, the myth of the solar Herakles was realised in some semi-historical prince of Argos and Mykenæ. Herakles may have been the name of the national god of the Heraklidæ, and this would explain the enmity of Hêrê, whose worship flourished in Argos before the Dorian immigration. What was formerly told of a god was transferred to Herakles, the leader of the Heraklidæ, the worshippers or sons of Herakles, while, at the same time, many local and historical facts connected with the Heraklidæ and their leaders may have been worked up with the myth of the divine hero. The idea of Herakles being, as it were, the bond-servant of Eurystheus is of solar origin—it is the idea of the sun fettered to his work, and toiling for men, his inferiors in strength and virtue. Thus Sîfrit is toiling for Gunther, and even Apollo is for one year the slave of Laomedon —pregnant expressions, necessitated by the absence of more abstract verbs, and familiar even to modern poets.

> ‘ As aptly suits therewith that modest pace
>   Submitted to the chains
>   That bind thee to the path which God
>   ordains
>   That thou shouldst trace.’
>   [—Wordsworth, *Thanksgiving Ode*, 1816.]

The later growth of epic and tragical poetry may be Greek, or Indian, or Teutonic ; it may take the different colours of the different skies, the different warmth of the different climes ; nay, it may attract and absorb much that is accidental and historical. But if we cut into it and analyse it, the blood that runs through all the ancient poetry is the same blood ; it is the ancient mythical speech. The atmosphere in which the early poetry of the Aryans grew up was mythological, it was impregnated with something that could not be resisted by those who breathed in it. It was like the siren voice of the modern rhyme, which has suggested so many common ideas to poets writing in a common language.

We know what Greek and Teutonic poets have made of their epic heroes ; let us see now whether the swarthy Hindu has been able to throw an equally beautiful haze around the names of his mythical traditions.

The story of the loves of Purûravas and Urvasî has frequently been told by Hindu poets. We find it in their epic poems, in their Purânas, and in the Brihat-kathâ, the *Great Story*, a collection of the popular legends of India. It has suffered many changes, yet even in Kalidâsa's [1] play, of which I shall give a short abstract, we recognise the distant background, and we may admire the skill with which this poet has breathed new life and human feeling into the withered names of a language long forgotten.

The first act opens with a scene in the Himâlaya mountains. The nymphs of heaven, on returning from an assembly of the gods, have been attacked, and are mourning over the loss of Urvasî, who has been carried off by a demon. King Purûravas enters on his chariot, and on hearing

[1] Professor Wilson has given the first and most beautiful translation of this play in his *Hindu Theatre*. The original was published first at Calcutta, and has since been reprinted several times. A very useful edition has lately [1856] been published by Professor Williams.

K

the cause of their grief, hastens to the rescue of the nymph. He soon returns, after having vanquished the robber, and restores Urvasî to her heavenly companions. But while he is carrying the nymph back to her friends in his chariot, he falls in love with her and she with him. He describes how he saw her slowly recovering from her terror :

> She recovers, though but faintly.
> So gently steals the moon upon the night,
> Retiring tardily ; so peeps the flame
> Of coming fires through smoky wreaths ; and
>   thus,
> The Ganges slowly clears her troubled wave,
> Engulphs the ruin that the crumbling bank
> Has hurled across her agitated course,
> And flows a clear and stately stream again.

When they part, Urvasî wishes to turn round once more to see Purûravas. She pretends that ' a straggling vine has caught her garland,' and, while feigning to disengage herself, she calls one of her friends to help her. Her friend replies :

> No easy task, I fear ; you seem entangled
> Too fast to be set free : but, come what may,
> Depend upon my friendship.'

The eye of the King then meets that of Urvasî, and he exclaims :

> A thousand thanks, dear plant, to whose kind aid
> I owe another instant, and behold
> But for a moment, and imperfectly,
> Those half-averted charms.

In the second act we meet the King at
Allahabad, his residence. He walks in the
garden of the palace, accompanied by a
Brahman, who acts the part of the gracioso
in the Indian drama. He is the confidential
companion of the King, and knows his love
for Urvasî. But he is so afraid of betraying
what must remain a secret to everybody at
court, and in particular to the Queen, that
he hides himself in a retired temple. There
a female servant of the Queen discovers
him, and ' as a secret can no more rest in
his breast than morning dew upon the
grass,' she soon finds out from him why the
King is so changed since his return from
the battle with the demon, and carries the
tale to the Queen. In the meantime, the
King is in despair, and pours out his grief:

Like one contending with the stream,
And still borne backwards by the current's force.

But Urvasî also is sighing for Purûravas,
and we suddenly see her, with her friend,
descending through the air to meet the King.
Both are at first invisible to him, and listen
to the confession of his love. Then Urvasî
writes a verse on a birch-leaf, and lets it
fall near the bower where her beloved reclines. Next, her friend becomes visible ;
and, at last, Urvasî herself is introduced to
the King. After a few moments, however,
both Urvasî and her friend are called back
by a messenger of the gods, and Purûravas

is left alone with his jester. He looks for the leaf on which Urvasî had first disclosed her love, but it is lost, carried away by the wind.

> Breeze of the south, the friend of love and
>   spring,
> Though from the flower you steal the fragrant
>   down
> To scatter perfume, yet why plunder me
> Of those dear characters, her own fair hand,
> In proof of her affection, traced ? Thou
>   knowest,
> The lonely lover that in absence pines,
> Lives on such fond memorials.

But worse than this, the leaf is picked up by the Queen, who comes to look for the King in the garden. There is a scene of matrimonial upbraiding, and, after a while, her majesty goes off in a hurry, like a river in the rains. The King is doubly miserable, for though he loves Urvasî, he acknowledges a respectful deference for his queen. At last he retires.

> 'Tis past mid-day, exhausted by the heat,
> The peacock plunges in the scanty pool,
> That feeds the tall tree's root : the drowsy bee
> Sleeps in the hollow chamber of the lotus,
> Darkened with closing petals ; on the brink
> Of the now tepid lake the wild duck lurks
> Amongst the sedgy shades ; and, even here,
> The parrot from his wiry bower complains,
> And calls for water to allay his thirst.

At the beginning of the third act we are first informed of what befell Urvasî, when she was recalled to Indra's heaven. She had to act before Indra—her part was that of the goddess of Beauty, who selects Vishnu for her husband. One of the names of Vishnu is Purushottama, and poor Urvasî, when called upon to confess whom she loves, forgetting the part she has to act, says, ' I love Purûravas,' instead of ' I love Purushottama.' The author of the play was so much exasperated by this mistake, that he pronounced a curse upon Urvasî, that she should lose her divine knowledge. But when the performance was over, Indra observing her as she stood apart, ashamed and disconsolate, called her. The mortal who engrossed her thoughts, he said, had been his friend in the hours of peril; he had aided him in conflict with the enemies of the gods, and was entitled to his acknowledgments. She must, accordingly, repair to the monarch, and remain with him ' till he beholds the offspring she shall bear him.'

A second scene opens, in the garden of the palace. The King has been engaged in the business of the state, and retires as the evening approaches.

> So ends the day, the anxious cares of state
> Have left no interval for private sorrow.
> But how to pass the night ? its dreary length
> Affords no promise of relief.

A messenger arrives from the Queen, apprising his majesty that she desires to see

him on the terrace of the pavilion. The
King obeys—and ascends the crystal steps
while the moon is just about to rise, and
the east is tinged with red.

King.—'Tis even so ; illumined by the rays
　　Of his yet unseen orb, the evening gloom
　　On either hand retires, and in the midst
　　The horizon glows, like a fair face that smiles
　　Betwixt the jetty curls on either brow
　　In clusters pendulous.　I could gaze for ever.

As he is waiting for the Queen, his desire
for Urvasî is awakened again :

　　　　In truth, my fond desire
　　Becomes more fervid as enjoyment seems
　　Remote, and fresh impediments obstruct
　　My happiness—like an impetuous torrent,
　　That, checked by adverse rocks, awhile delays
　　Its course, till high with chafing waters swollen
　　It rushes past with aggravated fury.
　　As spreads the moon its lustre, so my love
　　Grows with advancing night.

On a sudden Urvasî enters on a heavenly
car, accompanied by her friend.　They are
invisible again, and listen to the King ; but
the moment that Urvasî is about to withdraw her veil, the Queen appears.　She is
dressed in white, without any ornaments ;
and comes to propitiate her husband, by
taking a vow.

King.—In truth she pleases me.　Thus chastely
　　robed
　　In modest white, her clustering tresses decked

With sacred flowers alone, her haughty mien
Exchanged for meek devotion—thus arrayed
She moves with heightened charms.

Queen.—My gracious lord, I would perform a
    rite,
Of which you are the object, and must beg you
Bear with the inconvenience that my presence
May for brief time occasion you.

King.—You do me wrong ; your presence is a
    favour.
. . . Yet trust me, it is needless
To wear this tender form, as slight and delicate
As the lithe lotus stem, with rude austerity.
In me behold your slave, whom to propitiate
Claims not your care—your favour is his
    happiness.

Queen.—Not vain my vow, since it already
    wins me
My lord's complacent speech.

Then the Queen performs her solemn
vow ; she calls upon the god of the Moon:

Hear, and attest
The sacred promise that I make my husband !
Whatever nymph attract my lord's regard,
And share with him the mutual bonds of love,
I henceforth treat with kindness and com-
    placency.

The Brahman (the confidential friend of the
King), apart to Purûravas—The culprit that
escapes before his hand is cut off determines
never to run such a risk again. (Aloud) What
then ; is his majesty indifferent to your grace ?

Queen.—Wise sir, how think you—to promote
    his happiness
I have resigned my own. Does such a purpose
Prove him no longer dear to me ?

King.—I am not what you doubt me ; but the
    power
  Abides with you : do with me as you will.
  Give me to whom you please, or if you please,
  Retain me still your slave.

Queen.—Be what you list ;
  My vow is plighted—nor in vain the rite,
  If it afford you satisfaction. Come
  Hence, girls ; 'tis time we take our leave.

King.—Not so :
  So soon to leave me is no mark of favour.

Queen.—You must excuse me ; I may not
    forego
  The duties I have solemnly incurred.

It does not bring out the character of the
King under a very favourable light, that
this scene of matrimonial reconciliation,
when the Queen acts a part which we should
hardly expect on an oriental stage, should
be followed immediately by the apparition
of Urvasî. She has been present, though
invisible, during the preceding conversation
between him and his Queen, and she now
advances behind the King, and covers his
eyes with her hands.

It must be Urvasî (the king says) ;
No other hand could shed such ecstasy
Through this emaciate frame. The solar ray
Wakes not the night's fair blossom ; that alone
Expands when conscious of the moon's dear
    presence.[1]

---

[1] This refers to a very well-known legend. There
is one lotus which expands its flowers at the approach
of the sun and closes them during night. [Hence

Urvasî takes the resignation of the Queen in good earnest, and claims the King as granted her by right. Her friend takes leave, and she now remains with Purûravas as his beloved wife.

Urvasî.—I lament
  I caused my lord to suffer pain so long.
King.—Nay, say not so ! The joy that follows grief
  Gains richer zest from agony foregone.
  The traveller who, faint, pursues his track
  In the fierce day, alone can tell how sweet
  The grateful shelter of the friendly tree.

The next act is the gem of the whole play, though it is very difficult to imagine how it was performed without a *mise en scène* such as our modern theatres would hardly be able to afford. It is a melo-dramatic intermezzo, very different in style from the rest of the play. It is all in poetry, and in the most perfect and highly elaborate metres. Besides, it is not written in Sanskrit, but in Prakrit, the *lingua vulgaris* of India, poorer in form, but more melodious in sound than Sanskrit. Some

Harpocrates, the god of sunrise, was represented as an infant rising out of the lotus, the flower of Hades (Rawlinson, *Herodotus*, ii. 149; Wilkinson, *Ancient Egyptians*, ed. Birch, ii. 407), or of Nun, the primeval waters (Erman, *Handbook of Egyptian Religion*, 26 ; Maspero, *Dawn of Civilisation*, 146).] While another, the beloved of the moon, expands them during night and closes them during day-time. We have a similar myth of the *daisy*, the Anglo-Saxon *daeges edge*, day's eye, Wordsworth's darling.

of the verses are like airs to be performed by a chorus, but the stage directions which are given in the MSS. are so technical as to make their exact interpretation extremely difficult.

We first have a chorus of nymphs, deploring the fate of Urvasî. She had been living with the King in the groves of a forest, in undisturbed happiness.

Whilst wandering pleasantly along the brink
Of the Mandákini, a nymph of air,
Who gambolled on its sandy shore, attracted
The monarch's momentary glance—and this
Aroused the jealous wrath of Urvasî.
Thus incensed
She heedlessly forgot the law that bars
All female access from the hateful groves
Of Kârtikeya. Trespassing the bounds
Proscribed, she suffers now the penalty
Of her transgression, and, to a slender vine
Transformed, there pines till time shall set her
    free.

Mournful strains are heard in the air:

Soft voices low sound in the sky,
    Where the nymphs a companion deplore
And lament, as together they fly,
    The friend they encounter no more.
So sad and melodious awakes
    The plaint of the swan o'er the stream
When the red lotus blossoms, as breaks
    On the wave the day's orient beam.

Amidst the lake where the lotus, shining,
    Its flowers unfolds to the sunny beam,
The swan, for her lost companion pining,
    Swims sad and slow o'er the lonely stream.

The King now enters, his features expressing insanity, his dress disordered. The scene represents a wild forest, clouds gathering overhead, elephants, deer, peacocks, and swans are seen. Here are rocks and waterfalls, lightning and rain. The King first rushes frantically after a cloud which he mistakes for a demon that carried away his bride.

Hold, treacherous friend ; suspend thy flight—
    forbear :
Ah ! whither wouldst thou bear my beauteous
    bride ?
And now his arrows sting me ; thick as hail,
From yonder peak, whose sharp top pierces
    heaven,
They shower upon me,
        [*Rushes forward as to the attack, then
                pauses, and looks upwards.*]
It is no demon, but a friendly cloud—
No hostile quiver, but the bow of Indra ;
The cooling rain-drops fall, not barbed shafts,—
And I mistake the lightning for my love.

These raving strains are interrupted by airs, bewailing the fate of the separated lovers ; but it is impossible to give an idea of the real beauty of the whole, without much fuller extracts than we are able to give. The following passages may suffice :

Ah me ! whatever I behold but aggravates
My woe. These bright and pendulous flowers,
Surcharged with dew, resemble those dear eyes,
Glistening with starting tears. How shall I learn
If she have passed this way ?

He addresses various birds, and asks them whether they have seen his love, the peacock, ' the bird of the dark blue throat and eye of jet,'—the cuckoo, ' whom lovers deem Love's messenger,'—the swans, who are sailing northward, and ' whose elegant gait betrays that they have seen her,'—the *k*akravaka, a bird who, during the night, is himself separated from his mate—but none give answer. Neither he, nor the bees who murmur amidst the petals of the lotus, nor the royal elephant, that reclines with his mate under the kadamba tree, has seen the lost one.

King.—From his companion he accepts the bough,
    Her trunk has snapped from the balm-breathing tree—
    How rich with teeming shoots and juicy fragrance.
    He crushes it.
                Deep on the mountain's breast,
    A yawning chasm appears—such shades are ever
    Haunts of the nymphs of air and earth. Perchance,
    My Urvasî now lurks within the grotto,
    In cool seclusion. I will enter.—All
    Is utter darkness. Would the lightning's flash
    Now blaze to guide me— No, the cloud disdains—
    Such is my fate perverse—to shed for me
    Its many-channelled radiance. Be it so.
    I will retire—but first the rock address.

Air.

With horny hoofs and a resolute breast,
  The boar through the thicket stalks ;
He ploughs up the ground, as he plies his
    quest
  In the forest's gloomiest walks.

Say, mountain, whose expansive slope confines
The forest verge—oh tell me, hast thou seen
A nymph, as beauteous as the bride of love,
Mounting, with slender frame, thy steep
    ascent,
Or, wearied, resting in thy crowning woods ?
How ! no reply ? remote, he hears me not,—
I will approach him nearer.

Air.

From the crystal summits the glistening
    springs
  Rush down the flowery sides,
And the spirit of heaven delightedly sings,
  As among the peaks he hides.
Say, mountain so favoured—have the feet
Of my fair one pressed this calm retreat ?

Now, by my hopes, he answers ! He has
    seen her :
Where is she ?—say. Alas ! again deceived.
Alone I hear the echo of my words,
As round the cavern's hollow mouth they roll,
And multiplied return. Ah, Urvaṣî !
Fatigue has overcome me. I will rest
Upon the borders of this mountain torrent,
And gather vigour from the breeze that gleans
Refreshing coolness from its gelid waves.
Whilst gazing on the stream, whose new swoln
    waters
Yet turbid flow, what strange imaginings
Possess my soul, and fill it with delight.

The rippling wave is like her arching brow ;
The fluttering line of storks, her timid tongue ;
The foamy spray, her white loose floating robe ;
And this meandering course the current tracks,
Her undulating gait.   All these recall
My   soon-offended   love.   I   must   appease
      her. . . .
I'll back to where my love first disappeared.
Yonder the black deer couchant lies ; of him
I will inquire.   Oh, antelope, behold. . . .
How ! he averts his gaze, as if disdaining
To hear my suit !   Ah no, he, anxious, marks
His doe approach him ; tardily she comes,
Her frolic fawn impeding her advance.

At last the King finds a gem, of ruddy
radiance ; it is the gem of Union, which,
by its mighty spell, should restore Urvasî to
her lover.   He holds it in his hands, and
embraces the vine, which is now transformed into Urvasî.   The gem is placed on
Urvasî's forehead, and the King and his
heavenly Queen return to Allahabad.

                              Yonder cloud
Shall be our downy car, to waft us swift
And lightly on our way ; the lightning's wave
Its glittering banners ; and the bow of Indra
      (the rainbow)
Hangs as its over-arching canopy
Of variegated and resplendent hues.
                    [*Exeunt on the cloud.   Music.*]

The fifth and last act begins with an un-
lucky incident.   A hawk has borne away
the ruby of re-union.   Orders are sent to
shoot the thief, and, after a short pause, a

forester brings the jewel and the arrow by which the hawk was killed. An inscription is discovered on the shaft, which states that it belonged to Ayus, the son of Urvasî and Purûravas. The King is not aware that Urvasî has ever borne him a son ; but while he is still wondering, a female ascetic enters, leading a boy with a bow in his hand. It is Ayus, the son of Urvasî, whom his mother confided to the pious *K*yavana, who educated him in the forest, and now sends him back to his mother. The King soon recognises Ayus as his son. Urvasî also comes to embrace him :

Her gaze intent
Is fixed upon him, and her heaving bosom
Has rent its veiling scarf.

But why has she concealed the birth of this child ? and why is she now suddenly bursting into tears ? She tells the King herself:

When for your love I gladly left the courts
Of heaven, the Monarch thus declared his
will:
' Go, and be happy with the prince, my
friend ;
But when he views the son that thou shalt bear
him,
Then hitherward direct thy prompt return.' . . .
The fated term expires, and to console
His father for my loss, he is restored.
I may no longer tarry.

King.—The tree that languished in the summer's
     blaze
Puts forth, reviving, as young rain descends,
Its leafy shoots, when lo ! the lightning bursts
Fierce on its top, and fells it to the ground.

Urvasî.—But what remains for me ? my task
     on earth
Fulfilled.   Once gone, the King will soon
     forget me.

King.—Dearest, not so.   It is no grateful task
To tear our memory from those we love.
But we must bow to power supreme : do you
Obey your lord ; for me, I will resign
My throne to this my son, and with the deer
Will henceforth mourn amidst the lonely
     woods.

Preparations are made for the inaugura-
tion of the young king, when a new *deus ex
machina* appears—Narada, the messenger of
Indra.

Messenger.—May your days be many ! King,
     attend :
The mighty Indra, to whom all is known,
By me thus intimates his high commands.
Forego your purpose of ascetic sorrow,
And Urvasî shall be through life united
With thee in holy bonds.

After this all concludes happily.   Nymphs
descend from heaven with a golden vase
containing the water of the heavenly Ganges,
a throne, and other paraphernalia, which
they arrange.   The Prince is inaugurated as
partner of the empire, and all go together

to pay their homage to the Queen, who had so generously resigned her rights in favour of Urvaṣî, the heavenly nymph.

Here, then, we have the full flower, whose stem we trace through the Purâṇas and the Mahâbhárata to the Brâhmaṇas and the *Veda*, while the seed lies buried deep in that fertile stratum of language from which all the Aryan dialects draw their strength and nourishment. Mr. Carlyle had seen deep into the very heart of mythology when he said: 'Thus, though tradition may have but one root, it grows, like a banian, into a whole overarching labyrinth of trees.' The root of all the stories of Purûravas and Urvaṣî, were short proverbial expressions, of which ancient dialects are so fond. Thus: 'Urvaṣî loves Purûravas,' meant 'the sun rises'; 'Urvaṣî sees Purûravas naked,' meant 'the dawn is gone'; 'Urvaṣî finds Purûravas again,' meant 'the sun is setting.' The names of Purûravas and Urvaṣî are of Indian growth, and we cannot expect to find them identically the same in other Aryan dialects. But the same ideas pervade the mythological language of Greece. There one of the many names of the dawn was Eurydike (p. 128). The name of her husband is, like many Greek words, inexplicable, but Orpheus is the same word as the Sanskrit *R*ibhu or Arbhu, which, though it is best known as the name of the three *R*ibhus, was used in the *Veda* as an epithet

L

of Indra, and a name of the sun. The old story, then, was this : ' Eurydike is bitten by a serpent (*i.e.* by 'the night), she dies, and descends into the lower regions. Orpheus follows her, and obtains from the gods that his wife should follow him if he promised not to look back. Orpheus promises—ascends from the dark world below ; Eurydike is behind him as he rises, but, drawn by doubt or by love, he looks round ;—the first ray of the sun glances at the dawn, and the dawn fades away.' There may have been an old poet of the name of Orpheus—for old poets delight in solar names ; but, whether he existed or not, certain it is, that the story of Orpheus and Eurydike was neither borrowed from a real event, nor invented without provocation. In India also, the myth of the *R*ibhus has taken a local and historical colouring by a mere similarity of names. A man—or a tribe of the name of Bribu (*Rv.* vi. 46, 29) [1] was admitted into the Brahmanic community. They were carpenters, and had evidently rendered material assistance to Bharadvâga. As they had no Vaidik gods, the *R*ibhus were made over to them, and many things were ascribed to these gods which originally applied only to the mortal Bribus. These historical realities will never yield to a mythological analysis, while the truly mythological answers at once if we

[1] This explains the passage in *Manu*, x. 107, and shows how it ought to be corrected.

only know how to test it. There is a grammar by which this ancient dialect can be translated into the common language of the Aryans.

I must come to a close ; but it is difficult to leave a subject in which, as in an arch, each stone by itself threatens to fall, while the whole arch would stand the strongest pressure. One myth more.—We have seen how the sun and the dawn have suggested so many expressions of love, that we may well ask, did the Aryan nations, previous to their separation, know the most ancient of the gods, the god of Love ? Was *Eros* known at that distant period of awakening history, and what was meant by the name by which the Aryans called him ? The common etymology derives Eros from a Sanskrit root, vri or var, which means to choose, to select.

Now, if the name of Love had first been coined in our ballrooms, such an etymology might be defensible, but surely the idea of weighing, comparing, and prudently choosing could not have struck a strong and genuine heart as the most prominent feature of love, Let us imagine, as well as we can, the healthy and strong feelings of a youthful race of men, free to follow the call of their hearts—unfettered by the rules and prejudices of a refined society, and controlled only by those laws which nature and the graces have engraved on every human heart. Let us imagine such hearts suddenly lighted up by love—by a feeling of which they knew not either whence it came or where it would carry them ; an impulse they did not even know how to name. If they wanted a name for it, where could they look ? Was not love to them like an awakening from sleep ? Was it not like a morn radiating with heavenly splendour over their souls—pervading their hearts with a glowing warmth—purifying their whole being with a fresh breeze, and illuminating the whole world around them with a new light ? If it was so, there was but one name by which they could express love—there was but one similitude for the roseate bloom that betrays the dawn of love —it was the blush of the day—the rising of the sun. ' The sun has risen,' they said, where we say, ' I love '; ' the sun has set,' they said, where we say, ' I have loved.'

And this, which we might have guessed, if we could but throw off the fetters of our own language, is fully confirmed by an analysis of ancient speech. The name of the dawn in Sk. is ushas, the Greek 'Εως, both feminine. But the *Veda* knows also a masculine dawn, or rather a dawning sun (Agni aushasya, 'Εφος), and in this sense Ushas might be supposed to have taken in Greek the form of 'Ερως. S is frequently changed into r. In Sanskrit it is a general rule that s followed by a media becomes r. In Greek we have the Lakonic forms in oρ instead of os (Ahrens, D. D. § 8) ; in Latin, an r between two vowels often exists in ancient inscriptions under the more original form of s (*asa* = *ara*). The very word *ushas* has in Latin taken the form of *aurora*, which is derived from an intermediate *auros*, *auroris*, like *flora*, from *flos*, *floris*.

But, however plausible such analogies may seem, it is only throwing dust in our eyes if comparative philologists imagine they can establish in this manner the transition of a Sanskrit sh into a Greek r. No, whatever analogies other dialects may exhibit, no Sanskrit sh between two vowels has ever as yet been proved to be represented by a Greek r. Therefore Eros cannot be Ushas.

And yet Eros is the dawning sun. The sun in the *Veda* is frequently called the runner, the quick racer, or simply the horse,[1] while in the more humanised mythology of Greece, and also in many parts of the *Veda*, he is represented as standing on his cart, which in the *Veda* is drawn by two, seven, or ten horses, while in Greek we also have the quadriga :

Ἄρματα μὲν τάδε λαμπρὰ τεθρίππων
Ἥλιος ἤδη λάμπει κατὰ γῆν.

These horses are called Haritas ; they are always feminine. They are called bhadrâs, happy or joyful (i. 115, 3) ; *k*itrâ's, many-coloured (i. 115, 3) ; gh*r*itasnâs, bathed in

---

[1] [The horse was sacred to the sun, whose chariot he drew, among the Babylonians, Canaanites, Hebrews, Teutons, and other nations. See 2 Kings xxiii. 11.]

dew (iv. 6, 9); sva*n*kas, with beautiful steps; vîtap*r*ish*th*âs, with lovely backs (v. 45, 10). Thus we read:

Rv. ix. 63, 9.—The Sun has yoked the ten Harits for his journey.
Rv. i. 50, 8.—May the seven Harits bring the bright sun on thy cart.
Rv. iv. 13, 3.—The seven Harits bring him, the Sun, the spy of the world.

In other passages, however, they take a more human form, and as the Dawn which is sometimes called simply a*s*vâ, the marc, is well known by the name of the sister, these Harits also are called the Seven Sisters (vii. 66, 5); and in one passage (ix. 86, 37) they appear as ' the Harits with beautiful wings.' After this I need hardly say that we have here the prototype of the Grecian *Charites*.

I should like to follow the track which this recognition of the Charites, as the Sanskrit Haritas, opens to Comparative Mythology ; but I must return to Eros, in whose company they so frequently appear. If, according to the laws which regulate the metamorphosis of common Aryan words as adopted by Greek or Sanskrit, we transliterate ἔρως into Sanskrit, we find that its derivative suffix ως, ωτος, is the same as the termination of the participle of the perfect, and corresponds, therefore, to the Sanskrit vant ; nom. vâ (for vân), gen. vatas. There being no short e in Sanskrit, and a Greek ρ corresponding to a Sanskrit r, Ἔρως, ἔρωτος, if it existed at all in Sanskrit, would have had the form of A'rvân, árvatas. Now árvan in the later Sanskrit means only a horse, but in the *Veda* it has retained more of its radical power, and is used in the sense of quick running, vehement. It is frequently applied to the Sun, so that in some passages it stands as the name of the Sun, while in others it is used as a substantive, meaning horse or rider. Thus, through the irresistible influence of the synonymous character of ancient language, and without any poetical effort on the part of the speaker, those who spoke of the sun as arvan, spoke at the same time of a horse or rider. The word arvan, though intended only to express the rapid sun, set other ideas vibrating which gradually changed the sun into a horse or a horseman. Arvan means *horse* in passages like i. 91, 20—

The god Soma gives us the cow ; Soma gives us the quick horse ; Soma gives a strong son.

It means horseman, *Rv.* i. 132, 5—

The rider is born without a horse, without a bridle.

The rider who is meant here is the rising sun, and there is a whole hymn addressed to the sun as a horse. Nay, the growth of language and thought is so quick, that in the *Veda* the myth turns, so to speak, back upon itself ; and one of the poets (i. 163, 21)

praises the bright Vasus, because ' out of
the sun they have wrought a horse.'   Thus
árvan becomes by itself, without any adjective or explanation, the name for sun, like
sûrya, âditya, or any other of his old titles.
Rv. i. 163, 3, the poet tells the sun, ' Thou,
O Arvan (horse), art Aditya,' (the sun) ; and
(vi. 12, 6), Agni, or the sun, is invoked by
the same name : ' Thou, O Arvan, keep us
from evil report !   O Agni, lighted with all
the fires !   thou givest treasures, thou sendest
away all evils ; let us live happy for hundred
winters ; let us have good offspring.'

Before we can show how the threads of
this name of the Sun in India enters into
the first woof of the god of Love in Greece,
we have still to observe that sometimes the
horses, *i.e.* the rays of the sun, are called not
only Harítas, but rohítas and árushis.   *Rv.*
i. 14, 12, ' Yoke the A'rushîs to thy cart,
O bright Agni !   the Haríts, the Rohíts !   with
them bring the gods to us ! '   These names
may have been originally mere adjectives,
meaning white, bright, and brown,[1] but they
soon grew into names of certain animals
belonging to the gods, according to their

[1] Poi che l'altro mattin la bella Aurora
L'aer seren fe' bianco e rosso e giallo.
          —*Ariosto*, xxiii. 52.

Si che le bianche e le vermiglie guance,
Là dove io era, della bella Aurora
Per troppa etate divenivan rance.
          —Dante, *Purgatorio*, ii. 7.

different colour and character. Thus, we read :

Rv. ii. 10, 2.—Hear thou the brilliant Agni, my prayer ; whether the two black horses (syâvâ) bring thy cart, or the two brown (róhítâ) or the two white horses (arushâ).

And again :

Rv. vii. 42, 2.—Yoke the Haríts and the Rohíts, or the Arushás which are in thy stable.

As árvat was used for horse, árushî is used for cow ; for instance, viii. 55, 3, where a poet says he has received four hundred cows (árushînâm kátuh satám). These árushîs or bright cows, belong more particularly to the Dawn, and instead of saying ' the day dawns,' the old poets of the *Veda* say frequently, ' the bright cows return ' (*Rv.* i. 92, 1). We found that the Haríts were sometimes changed into seven sisters, and thus the A'rushîs also, originally the bright cows, underwent the same metamorphosis.

Rv. x. 5, 5.—The seven sisters, the A'rushîs (the bright cows) knew of the sun : or (x. 8, 3) —When the sun flew up the A'rushîs refreshed their bodies in the water.

Sanskrit scholars hardly need to be told that this árushî is in reality the feminine of arvâ, or arvân, though there is also another form of the feminine, árvatî. As vidvâ'n, knowing, forms its feminine vidúshî, (*k*ikitvā'n, *k*ikitúshî) so árvâ(*n*) makes árushî, a form which fully explains the formation of the feminine of the past participle in Greek. This may be shown by the following equation : vidvâ'n : vidúshî = εἰδώς : εἰδυῖα. The transition of árvâ into árushî is important for our purpose, because it throws new light on the origin of another word derived from arvat, the sun ; and this is arushá, a masculine, and in the *Veda* again, one of the most frequent epithets or names of the sun. Arushá, gen. àsya, follows the weak declension, and is formed like διάκτορος, ου, instead of διάκτωρ, ορος ; like Lat. *vasum, i*, instead of *vas, vasis ;* like Prakrit *k*aranteshu instead of *k*aratsu, like Mod. Greek ἡ νύκτα, instead of ἡ νύξ. Sanskrit scholars will best understand this by the following equation:

árvâ (running) : árus : arushá = párva (knot) :
    párus : parushá.

This arushá, as used in the *Veda*,[1] brings us as near to the Greek Eros as we can expect ; for arushá is used in the sense of bright.

Rv. vii. 75, 6.—The bright spotted horses are seen bringing to us the brilliant Dawn.

---

[1] [See a fuller discussion of the word in M. Müller's *Rig-Veda-Sanhita*, vol. i. pp. 6-15, but his theory won no acceptance. *Erôs* seems to have meant radically impetuosity and then eager desire, from the root *ar*, to run or rush, whence Vedic *arvat*, a runner, (1) a horse, (2) the sun—Curtius, i. 139.]

The horses [1] of Indra, of Agni, of Br̄ihaspati, as quick as the wind, and as bright as suns, who lick the udder of the dark cow, the night, are called arushá ; the smoke which rises from the burning sun at daybreak, the limbs of the sun with which he climbs the sky, the thunderbolt which Indra throws, the fire which is seen by day and by night, all are called arushá. ' He who fills heaven and earth with light, who runs across darkness along the sky, who is seen among the black cows of the night,' he is called arushá or the bright bull (arushó vr̄íshâ).

But this very *Arusha* is in the *Veda*, as in Greek mythology, represented as a child.

Rv. iii. 1, 4.—The Seven Sisters have nursed him, the joyful, the white one, as he was born, Arusha, with great might ; as horses go to the foal that is born, so did the gods bring up the sun when he was born.

Arusha is always the young sun in the *Veda ;* the sun who drives away the dark night, and sends his first rays to awaken the world.

Rv. vii. 71, 1.—Night goes away from her sister Dawn, the dark one opens the path for Arusha.

Though in some of his names there is an unintentional allusion to his animal char-

[1] Arusha, si voisin d'Aruna (cocher du soleil), et d'Arus (le soleil), se retrouve en Zend sous la forme d'Aurusha (dont Anquetil fait Eorosh, l'oiseau), les chevaux qui trainent Serosh.—Burnouf, *Bhag. Pur.* LXXIX.

acter, he soon takes a purely human form. He is called Nrikakshâs (iii. 15, 3), 'having the eyes of a man,' and even his wings, as Grimm [1] will be glad to learn, have commenced to grow, in the *Veda*, where once (v. 47, 3) he is called ' Arusháh suparnás,' ' the bright sun with beautiful wings.' [2]

Τὸν δ' ἤτοι θνητοὶ μὲν "Ερωτα καλοῦσι ποτηνόν,
'Αθάνατοι δε Πτέρωτα, διὰ πτεροφύτορ' ἀνάγκην.

As Eros is the child of Zeus, Arusha is called the child of Dyaus (Diváh sísus).

Rv. vii. 15, 6.—Him, the god Agni, they adorn and purify every day like a horse that has run his race—like Arushá, the bright sun, the young child of Dyaus (heaven).

Rv. vi. 49, 2.—Let us worship Agni, the child of heaven, the son of strength, Arushá, the bright light of the sacrifice.

This child is the first of the gods, for he comes (v. 1, 5) ' agre ahnâm,' at the point of the days ; ' ushasâm agre,' (x. 45, 5) at the beginning of the dawns ; but in one passage two daughters are ascribed to him— different in appearance—the one decked with the stars, the other brilliant by the light of the sun—Day and Night, who are elsewhere called the daughters of the Sun. As the god of Love, in the Greek sense of the word, Arusha does not occur, neither

[1] See Jacob Grimm's *Essay on the God of Love.*

[2] [Compare the sun disk with extended wings, a symbol very widely diffused in antiquity, and the wings of the sun in Malachi, iv. 2 ; the Vedic "head with wings," *supra*, 111.]

has love, as a mere feeling, been deified in the *Veda* under any name. Kâma, who is the god of Love in the later Sanskrit, never occurs in the *Veda* with personal or divine attributes, except in one passage of the 10th book, and here love is rather represented as a power of creation than as a personal being. But there is one other passage in the *Veda*, where Kâma, love, is clearly applied to the rising sun. The whole hymn (ii. 38, 6) is addressed to Savitar, the sun. It is said, 'he rises as a mighty flame—he stretches out his wide arms—he is even like the wind. When he stops his horses, all activity ceases, and the night follows in his track. But before she has half finished her weaving, the sun rises again. Then Agni goes to all men and to all houses; his light is powerful, and his mother, the Dawn, gives him the best share, the first worship among men.' Then the poet goes on :—

He came back, with wide strides, longing for victory ; the love of all men came near. The eternal approached, leaving the work (of Night) half-done ; he followed the command of the heavenly Savitar.

' The love of all men,' may mean he who is loved by all men, or who grants their wishes to all men ; yet I do not think it is by accident that Kâma, love, is thus applied to the rising sun.

Nor was the original solar character of the god of Love, the beloved of the Dawn, forgotten even in the later traditions of the Purânas. For we find that one of the names given to the son of Kâma, to Aniruddha, the irresistible (ἀνίκατος μάχαν), is Ushâpati, the lord of the Dawn.

If we place clearly before our mind all the ideas and allusions which have clustered round the name of Arvat and Arusha in the *Veda*, the various myths told of Eros, which at first seem so contradictory, become perfectly intelligible. He is in Hesiod the oldest of the gods, born when there is as yet only Chaos and Earth. Here we have ' Arusha born at the beginning of all the days.' He is the youngest of the gods, the son of Zeus, the friend of the Charites, also the son of the chief Charis, Aphrodite, in whom we can hardly fail to discover a female Eros (an Ushâ instead of an Agni aushasya). Every one of these myths finds its key in the *Veda*. He is there ' the child, the son of Dyaus ; he yokes the Harits, and is, if not the son,[1] at least the beloved of the dawn.' Besides, in Greek mythology also, Eros has many fathers and many mothers ; and one pair of parents given him by Sappho, Heaven and Earth, is identical with his Vaidik parents, Dyaus and Idâ. India, however, is not Greece, and though we may

[1] *Cf.* Maxim. Tyr. XXIV., τὸν Ἔρωτά φησιν ἡ Διοτίμα τῷ Σωκράτει οὐ παῖδα, ἀλλ᾽ ἀκόλουθον τῆς Ἀφροδίτης καὶ θεράποντα εἶναι. See Preller, *Greek Mythology*, p. 238.

trace the germs and roots of Greek words
and Greek ideas to the rich soil of India,
the full flower of Aryan language, of Aryan
poetry and mythology, belongs to Hellas,
where Plato has told us what Eros is, and
where Sophokles sang his

> Ἔρως ἀνίκατε μάχαν,
> Ἔρως, ὃς ἐν κτήμασι πίπτεις
> ὃς ἐν μαλακαῖς παρειαῖς
> νεάνιδος ἐννυχεύεις·
> φοιτᾷς δ' ὑπερπόντιος, ἐν τ'
> ἀγρονόμοις αὐλαῖς·
> καί σ' οὔτ' ἀθανάτων φύξιμος οὐδεὶς
> οὔθ' ἀμερίων ἐπ' ἀν-
> θρώπων· ὁ δ' ἔχων μέμηνεν.
>
> [*Antigone*, ll. 775–790, ed. Wunder.]

[O Love, 'gainst whom we fight in vain ;
O Love, who on thy victims fall'st with might,
  And yet thou slumberest all night
  In the soft cheeks of maidenhood.
Thou roamest far away beyond the seas,
And dwellest at home in rustic cottages ;
  None of the gods' immortal breed
  Nor yet of men shortlived
  Has e'er escaped from thee ;
  And he whom thou dost seize
  Goes straightway mad.] [1]

---

[1] [A curiously similar passage occurs in Steele's *The
Lover*, 1714 : "Among all the passions, to which the
frailty and weakness of man subject him, there is not
any that extends such a boundless and despotick Empire
over the whole species, as that of Love. . . . This has
subdued the exalted minds of the most aspiring tyrants,
and has melted the most sanguine complexion into an
effeminate softness. The mighty Hercules let fall his
club at a woman's feet. The scholar, the statesman,
and the soldier have all been lovers, and the most
ignorant swain has neglected both his flocks and pipe
to woo Daphne or Sylvia' (No. 25).]

If Hegel calls the discovery of the common origin of Greek and Sanskrit the discovery of a new world, the same may be said with regard to the common origin of Greek and Sanskrit mythology. The discovery is made, and the science of comparative mythology will soon rise to the same importance as comparative philology. I have here explained but a few myths, but they all belong to one small cycle, and many more names might have been added. I may refer those who take an interest in the geology of language to the *Journal of Comparative Philology*, published by my learned friend, Dr. Kuhn, at Berlin, who, in his periodical, has very properly admitted comparative mythology as an integral part of comparative philology, and who has himself discovered some striking parallelisms between the traditions of the *Veda* and the mythological names of the other Aryan nations. The very ' Hippokentaurs and the Chimæra, the Gorgons and Pegasos, and other monstrous creatures,' have been set right ; and though I do not hold Dr. Kuhn's views on many points, and particularly with regard to the elementary character of the gods, which he, like Lauer, the lamented author of the *System of Greek Mythology*, connects too exclusively with the fleeting phenomena of clouds, and storms, and thunder, while I believe their original conception to have been almost always solar,

yet there is much to be learnt from both,
even where we cannot agree with their conclusions. Much, no doubt, remains to be
done, and even with the assistance of the
Veda, the whole of Greek mythology will
never be deciphered and translated. But can
this be urged as an objection ? There are
many Greek words of which we cannot find a
satisfactory etymology, even by the help of
Sanskrit. Are we therefore to say that the
whole Greek language has no etymological
organisation ? If we find a rational principle in the formation of but a small portion
of Greek words, we are justified in inferring
that the same principle which manifests
itself in part governed the organic growth
of the whole ; and though we cannot explain
the etymological origin of all words, we
should never say that language had no etymological origin, or that etymology ' treats of
a past which was never present.' That the
later Greeks, such as Homer and Hesiod,
ignored the λόγος of their μύθοι I fully
admit, but they equally ignored the real
origin (τὸ ἔτυμον) of their words. What
applies to etymology, therefore, applies with
equal force to mythology. It has been
proved by comparative philology that there
is nothing irregular in language, and what
was formerly considered as irregular in declension and conjugation is now recognised
as the most regular and primitive formation
of grammar. The same, we hope, may be

M

accomplished in mythology, and instead of deriving it, as heretofore, ' ab ingenii humani imbecillitate et a dictionis egestate,' it will obtain its truer solution, ' ab ingenii humani sapientia et a dictionis abundantia.' Myth* ology is only a dialect, an ancient form of language. Mythology, though chiefly con-cerned with nature, and here again mostly with those manifestations which bear the character of law, order, power, and wisdom impressed on them, was applicable to all things. Nothing is excluded from mytho-logical expression ; neither morals nor philo-sophy, neither history nor religion, have escaped the spell of that ancient sibyl. But mythology is neither philosophy, nor his-tory, nor religion, nor ethics. It is, if we may use a scholastic expression, a *quale,* not a *quid*—something formal, not some-thing substantial, and, like poetry, sculp-ture, and painting, applicable to nearly all that the ancient world could admire or adore.

INDEX

INDEX

ABSTRACT words, 70–73
Aes, 59
Aeschylos, quoted, 20
Ahan, 117
Allegory, 86
Am, 79
Antiquity, interest of, 8
Arachne, 59
Aranea, 59
Arare, 54
Ardita, 36
Argentum, 59
Arusha, 170–172
Arushis, 169
Arvan, 167
Arvat, 169
Aryan, common words, 48–65
Ἄστυ, 52
Asvins, 119
Auxiliary verbs, 78
Aver, 35
Avunculus, 43

Βασιλεύει ἥλιος, 97
Bear, 54
Bitto and Phainis, 13
Bos, 36
Bo-sluaiged, 35
Boukólos, 36
Brâhmana, quoted, 130–132
Brother, 28, 32
Brynhildhr, 139–140

CARLYLE, quoted, 161
Charites, 166
Childhood of the World, 9
Comparative philology, 95, 96
Corn, 57
Cousin, 44
Cow, 36

Δαήρ, 68, 69
Dah, 117
Daphne, 119, 120
Dasa-pati, 50
Daughter, 28, 32, 33
Dawn, 117, 121, 137
Day, 117
Decimal system, 63, 64
Delios, 94
Despot, 50
Dialectical period, 12
Dioskuroi, 119
Domus, 51
Door, 52
Duh, 33

EARTH, synonyms of, 92
Endymion, 102–106, 108
Ensis, 60
Eôs, 164
Erinyes, 90
Eros, myth of, 90, 163
Europe, 128
Eurydike, 162

THE END

Printed by BALLANTYNE, HANSON & Co.
Edinburgh & London

INTERNATIONAL FOLKLORE

An Arno Press Collection

Allies, Jabez. **On The Ancient British, Roman, and Saxon Antiquities and Folk-Lore of Worcestershire.** 1852

Blair, Walter and Franklin J. Meine, editors. **Half Horse Half Alligator.** 1956

Bompas, Cecil Henry, translator. **Folklore of the Santal Parganas.** 1909

Bourne, Henry. **Antiquitates Vulgares; Or, The Antiquities of the Common People.** 1725

Briggs, Katharine Mary. **The Anatomy of Puck.** 1959

Briggs, Katharine Mary. **Pale Hecate's Team.** 1962

Brown, Robert. **Semitic Influence in Hellenic Mythology.** 1898

Busk, Rachel Harriette. **The Folk-Songs of Italy.** 1887

Carey, George. **A Faraway Time and Place.** 1971

Christiansen, Reidar Th. **The Migratory Legends.** 1958

Clouston, William Alexander. **Flowers From a Persian Garden, and Other Papers.** 1890

Colcord, Joanna Carver. **Sea Language Comes Ashore.** 1945

Dorson, Richard Mercer, editor. **Davy Crockett.** 1939

Douglas, George Brisbane, editor. **Scottish Fairy and Folk Tales.** 1901

Gaidoz, Henri and Paul Sébillot. **Blason Populaire De La France.** 1884

Gardner, Emelyn Elizabeth. **Folklore From the Schoharie Hills, New York.** 1937

Gill, William Wyatt. **Myths and Songs From The South Pacific.** 1876

Gomme, George Laurence. **Folk-Lore Relics of Early Village Life.** 1883

Grimm, Jacob and Wilhelm. **Deutsche Sagen.** 1891

Gromme, Francis Hindes. **Gypsy Folk-Tales.** 1899

Hambruch, Paul. **Faraulip.** 1924

Ives, Edward Dawson. **Larry Gorman.** 1964

Jansen, William Hugh. **Abraham "Oregon" Smith.** 1977

Jenkins, John Geraint. **Studies in Folk Life.** 1969

Kingscote, Georgiana and Pandit Natêsá Sástrî, compilers. **Tales of the Sun.** 1890

Knowles, James Hinton. **Folk-Tales of Kashmir.** 1893

Lee, Hector Haight. **The Three Nephites.** 1949

MacDougall, James, compiler. **Folk Tales and Fairy Lore in Gaelic and English.** 1910

Mather, Increase. **Remarkable Providences Illustrative of the Earlier Days of American Colonisation.** 1856

McNair, John F.A. and Thomas Lambert Barlow. **Oral Tradition From the Indus.** 1908

McPherson, Joseph McKenzie. **Primitive Beliefs in the North-East of Scotland.** 1929

Miller, Hugh. **Scenes and Legends of the North of Scotland.** 1869

Müller, Friedrich Max. **Comparative Mythology.** 1909

Palmer, Abram Smythe. **The Samson-Saga and Its Place in Comparative Religion.** 1913

Parker, Henry. **Village Folk-Tales of Ceylon.** Three volumes. 1910-1914

Parkinson, Thomas. **Yorkshire Legends and Traditions.** 1888

Perrault, Charles. **Popular Tales.** 1888

Rael, Juan B. **Cuentos Españoles de Colorado y Nuevo Méjico.** Two volumes. 1957

Ralston, William Ralston Shedden. **Russian Folk-Tales.** 1873

Rhys Davids, Thomas William, translator. **Buddhist Birth Stories; Or, Jātaka Tales.** 1880

Ricks, George Robinson. **Some Aspects of the Religious Music of the United States Negro.** 1977

Swynnerton, Charles. **Indian Nights' Entertainment, Or Folk-Tales From the Upper Indus.** 1892

Sydow, Carl Wilhelm von. **Selected Papers on Folklore.** 1948

Taliaferro, Harden E. **Fisher's River (North Carolina) Scenes and Characters.** 1859

Temple, Richard Carnac. **The Legends of the Panjâb.** Three volumes. 1884-1903

Tully, Marjorie F. and Juan B. Rael. **An Annotated Bibliography of Spanish Folklore in New Mexico and Southern Colorado.** 1950

Wratislaw, Albert Henry, translator. **Sixty Folk-Tales From Exclusively Slavonic Sources.** 1889

Yates, Norris W. **William T. Porter and the Spirit of the Times.** 1957